AF302675

Dr. Miroslav Stimac

The desktop operating system Haiku

Analysis of the operating system with focuses on

ease of use, GUI, multimedia capability

and an empirical research of the Haiku community

Master thesis

FernUniversität Hagen

2011

Bibliografische Information der Deutschen Nationalbibliothek

Die Deutsche Nationalbibliothek verzeichnet diese Publikation in der Deutschen Nationalbibliografie; detaillierte bibliografische Daten sind im Internet über http://dnb.d-nb.de abrufbar.

1. Aufl. - Göttingen : Cuvillier, 2011

978-3-86955-835-6

The image on the front cover was designed by Miroslav Stimac. Special thanks to my parents, Marijan and Mirjana Stimac, who had the idea for the front cover.

© CUVILLIER VERLAG, Göttingen 2011
    Nonnenstieg 8, 37075 Göttingen
    Telefon: 0551-54724-0
    Telefax: 0551-54724-21
    www.cuvillier.de

Abstract

Haiku is an open source, light, fast and user-friendly operating system that is inspired by the "Multimedia Operating System" BeOS. At the moment Haiku is still under development and the latest release was Alpha 2 which is meant to be used only for testing. Unlike many other open source operating systems, such as Linux or FreeBSD, Haiku sets the focus on personal computing and the graphic user interface (GUI) is not just an "Add-On" or "additional windows management system" but it is an essential part of the kernel.

This thesis analyses Haiku, especially regarding the ease of use, the GUI and the multimedia capabilities, by giving an introduction to Haiku, an overview of the history and features of BeOS and a lot of general and technical information about the architecture, the easy of use, the GUI and some other aspects of operating systems in general respectively in the special case of Haiku.

In order to recognize the main fields of application of Haiku and the expectations of the users regarding the further development of Haiku, the Haiku community has been analysed by doing an online survey that was answered by more than one thousand persons.

In summary, the author brings forward the arguments that Haiku could become a powerful, light and user-friendly operating system, but currently there is a lack of compatible modern multimedia software products and drivers for many multimedia devices. The outcome of this is that Haiku will not become a powerful multimedia operating system in near future, but it could become a user-friendly and very fast operating system for low-budget PCs and netbooks.

Acknowledgements

Hereby I want to say

THANK YOU

to the Haiku community and all people that answered my survey!

Special thanks to:

- Axel Dörfler because he added a link to my survey on the official Haiku website (haiku-os.org).
- Humdinger (the web administrator of haiku-gazette.de) because he added a link to my survey on his website.
- Christian Icking and Lihong Ma because of their wonderful course "Betriebssysteme" (operating systems), my first course at the FernUniversitaet Hagen, that inspired me to write this master thesis.
- My parents, Marijan and Mirjana, who supported me with their love and motivating words.

<u>List of tables:</u>

<u>List of graphics</u>

<u>**Page**</u>

<u>List of abbreviations</u>

Abbreviation	Meaning
AMD	Advanced Micro Devices
API	Application Programming Interface
ARM	Advanced RISC (Reduced Instruction Set Computer) Machine
ASP	Active Server Pages
BFS	Be File System
BSD	Berkeley Software Distribution
C64	Commodore 64 (a home computer)
CSS	Cascading Style Sheet
e.g.	Exempli gratia (Latin), for example
FAT	File Allocation Table (file system)
FAT32	32 bit File Allocation Table (file system)
FPS	Frames Per Second

GB	Gigabyte
GHz	Gigahertz
GUI	Graphic User Interface
HTML	Hyper Text Markup Language
ISO	International Organisation for Standardization
MB	Megabyte
MHz	Megahertz
MIDI	Musical Instrument Digital Interface
MIP	Multichannel Interface Processor
NTFS	New Technology File System
OpenGL	Open Graphics Library
OS	Operating System
p.	Page or pages
PATA	Parallel Advanced Technology Attachment, a hard disk interface
PCI	Peripheral Component Interconnect, a widely used input/output bus in many computers.
POP	Post Office Protocol
POSIX	Portable Operating System Interface for Unix
RPS	Rotations Per Second
RS232 or RS-232	Recommended Standard 232 (computer serial interface, IEEE)
s.	See, second or seconds
SATA	Serial Advanced Technology Attachment, a hard disk interface
SMTP	Simple Mail Transfer Protocol
SPSS	Statistical Package for the Social Sciences
SQL	Structured Query Language for data bases
USB	Universal Serial Bus
TB	Terabyte
VBS	Visual Basic Script
WiFi or Wi-Fi	Wireless Fidelity (IEEE 802.11b wireless networking)

A. Introduction

What is the most important difference between personal computers nowadays?

While there had been many different hardware platforms for personal computers in the 1980s and the first half of the 1990s, for example the famous home computers such as the Commodore 64, Commodore 128, Amiga or Atari ST, today most of the personal computers are based on the same hardware architecture: they are x86 compatible and contain in most cases a processor from Intel or AMD. Even Apple installs x86 compatible processors in most of their new computer systems.

When we take a look at the interfaces for the graphic cards and peripheral devices, so we recognize that there are also standards which dominate the market. For example, think about the PCI bus and the USB interface.

Nowadays the most important difference between the personal computers is not the hardware architecture but it is the operating system which is installed by the manufacturer or the user.

The leader in the market is Microsoft with the Windows operating systems, followed by Apple Mac OS X, Linux, FreeBSD, Unix and a large number of other not very well known operating systems.

Most of the well known operating systems are not free. Only some Linux and FreeBSD distributions are free for private purposes, but both operating systems are mostly used for server systems and are very rare on desktop clients because many Linux and FreeBSD distributions are not very easy to use and a great number of ordinary users is deterred or confused.

In opposite to Linux and FreeBSD, Haiku is meant to be a very end-user friendly operating system that specially targets personal computing.

"Haiku is a fast, efficient, easy to use and learn open source operating system inspired by the BeOS that specifically targets personal computing. It is also the name of the project that develops and promotes Haiku the operating system."[1]

Perhaps you already heard the term Haiku in literature. Haiku is a classical Japanese poetry form and belongs to the most important poetry forms from Japan. It is a simple and very short poetry form. Nowadays a Haiku poem has three lines of five, seven and five syllables. The form of five-

---

[1] *Quotation: Haiku, Inc.: What is Haiku?, in the internet: http://www.haiku-os.org/about/faq, Date: 19th June 2010*

seven-five syllables is a must in Japanese[2], but in the English language, which is not based on syllables, it is not always easy to fulfil this requirement.

An old pond!

A frog jumps in-

The sound of water.

(A Haiku written by Matsuo Basho, 1644-1694)[3]

A Haiku shall paint a clear picture that contains only the most important elements and aspects of something. The topic of a Haiku is often from the daily life, about feelings, nature, work or daily experiences.

The operating system Haiku was named after this Japanese form of poetry to express the simplicity and user-friendliness of the operating system from the point of view of the users:

"Haiku is named after the classical three-line Japanese poetry form. Haiku poetry is known for its quiet power, elegance and simplicity - among the core qualities of BeOS which we aim to recreate in Haiku. BeOS included some haiku in its user interface, in the form of network error messages displayed by its web browser. An example:

Sites you are seeking

From your path they are fleeing

Their winter has come.

While there are no current plans to include poetic messages in Haiku, we consider this another subtle way of proudly cherishing our BeOS roots."[4]

From the point of view of the end-users the graphic user interface (GUI) plays a major role regarding software ergonomics.

For users that are not very versed in technology the GUI seems to be the most important component

---

2 *Japanese words consist of syllables and vowels. Therefore Japanese sounds very harmonic and melodic.*

3 *Toyomasu, K. G.: HAIKU for PEOPLE, in the internet: http://www.toyomasu.com/haiku, last updated: 10th January 2001, Date: 14th August 2010*

4 *Quotation: Haiku, Inc.: General FAQ: Where does the name Haiku come from?, in the Internet: http://www.haiku-os.org/about/faq, Date: 24th July 2010*

of the operating system, perhaps they even identify the operating systems only by looking at the graphic user interface.

Haiku is inspired by BeOS, which is often also called the Multimedia OS because it was very advanced and powerful in fields of multimedia, audio and video editing in the past when competitors such as Windows 95 were very unstable when trying to simultaneously play several video clips (see chapter 1).

Just like BeOS, Haiku also sets a focus on multimedia capabilities because most ordinary end-users need their personal computers not only for classic purposes such as writing letters and working, but they also need them for listening to music, watching video clips, editing photographies and private video recordings. Therefore the multimedia capabilities are a very important feature of a desktop operating system which targets personal computing.

Because of the above mentioned aspects, among other things the graphic user interface and the multimedia capabilities of Haiku will be analysed and discussed in this master thesis. In so doing, the focuses will be set on both: the psychological aspects of software ergonomics and the technological aspects (see chapter 5). These questionings will be set in the foreground:

- Which aspects of design are important for the usability of a graphic user interface? Which of these aspects are implemented in the graphic user interface of Haiku?
- What is the performance of the graphic user interface, especially the response time regarding the interactivity with the user?
- Is the graphic system powerful regarding multimedia applications and games?
- How does the technical implementation regarding music and sound look like?
- What are the advantages and disadvantages of the Haiku graphic user interface and the graphic system?
- Are the structure and the documentations of those components, that are relevant for the multimedia capabilities and the development of the graphic user interface, attractive from the point of view of software developers?

The chapters 5 and 6 are the most important parts of this master thesis.

In the chapter 6 the results of an empirical research are presented. The data source of this empirical study is my online survey which is designed to research the Haiku community. The main goals of this empirical study are:

- The analysis and clustering of the members of the Haiku community regarding their sociodemographic characteristics and their information technology background.
- To find out why the members of the Haiku community are interested in Haiku.
- It is interesting to find out how people use Haiku and what are the most important purposes.
- The identification of the expectations of the users regarding Haiku.

For many readers of this thesis Haiku is an unknown operating system. Therefore it will be introduced in the first three chapters. These chapters do not belong to the most important parts of this thesis, but they are important to give the reader an opportunity to holistically understand the Haiku operating system.

My thesis is that Haiku could become a popular, user-friendly and fast desktop operating system that has only low hardware requirements and can be used in cheap PCs, notebooks and netbooks.

I will explain my thesis by giving further information in the chapter 4 and test it by analysing the user-friendliness and the multimedia capabilities of Haiku in the chapter 5 and researching the Haiku community in the chapter 6.

From my point of view, Haiku is already now a very user-friendly and fast operating system, although it is only an Alpha version and there are still many problems that will be hopefully solved in the next few years. Furthermore, I will explain why I think that Haiku is not a powerful multimedia operating system at the moment, but it could perhaps become very powerful in fields of multimedia and games in the future.

B. Main part

1. Haiku, the successor of BeOS?

As already mentioned in the introduction, the Haiku Inc. says that Haiku is inspired by BeOS: "Haiku is a fast, efficient, easy to use and learn open source operating system **inspired by the BeOS** that specifically targets personal computing. It is also the name of the project that develops and promotes Haiku the operating system."[5]

In fact, Haiku is a try to create a BeOS like operating system from scratch. Haiku looks and feels almost like BeOS and it is more or less compatible with BeOS. This means that not all, but some software, that runs in BeOS, will also run in Haiku. Nevertheless, Haiku is more than just BeOS because Haiku contains many drivers for modern hardware devices and supports some current technologies. For example, there are versions of Haiku which are built with GCC4, which was not available in BeOS.

In the following subchapters you will get a short overview of the history of BeOS, Haiku and other related operating systems. Furthermore, you will have the opportunity to learn about the similarities and differences between BeOS and Haiku.

---

5 *Quotation: Haiku, Inc.: What is Haiku?, in the Internet: http://www.haiku-os.org/about/faq,
Date: 19th June 2010*

1.1. The history of BeOS and Haiku

The operating system BeOS was developed by the company Be and Jean-Louis Gassée, who was before employed at Apple. The development of the operating system begun in 1990.

In the early stages BeOS was designed for a special hardware, the BeBox, which was to contain dual RISC processors (Motorola 88110s). This operating system, which could be described as an ancestor or a very early version of BeOS, already had a focus on multimedia performance.[6]

In the following years the next versions of BeOS were developed for PowerPC and x86 compatible personal computers.

Release date	Release	Comments
First half of the 1990s.	DR1 – DR5	Little known. Hobbit, possible BeBox.
January 1996	DR6	The first widely used developer edition. BeBox.
April 1996	DR7	The second widely used developer edition. BeBox.
September 1996	DR8	Mac and BeBox.
May 1997	BeOS preview release.	
March 1998	BeOS 3.0 x86 version.	
April 1998	BeOS 3.0 PowerPC version.	
June 1998	BeOS 3.1	
July 1998	BeOS 3.2	Better hardware support (SCSI) and about 800 software products are available.
November 1998	BeOS 4.0	Available for PCs and Macs.
1999	BeOS 4.1	Integration of the instruction set SIMD of the processor Intel Pentium III.
June 1999	BeOS 4.5	Also called Genki. Available for PPC/Intel.

---

6 *Hacker, S. / Bortman, H. / Herborth, C. (1999): The BeOS Bible, Peachpit Press, California, pages 31 and 32.*

| March 2000 | BeOS 5.0 | Also called Maui. Two editions were available, the Pro and the Personal edition. PPC/Intel. |

Table 1: Some important milestones in the history of BeOS[7]

In November 2001 the Be Inc. was acquired by Palm and the development of BeOS was stopped.

As already mentioned, Haiku is a successor of BeOS. But Haiku is not the only one operating system that was inspired by BeOS. There were some other projects and operating systems that tried to continue the path that BeOS begun to walk on.

The most popular ones were BlueEyedOS, Zeta and OpenBeOS.

Zeta is a commercial operating system developed by the company yellowTAB and distributed by the company magnussoft Deutschland GmbH. Zeta is a successor of the BeOS Personal Edition, which was a BeOS distribution of the company Be and it was meant for personal usage, with source code from the OpenBeOS project.[8]

On 5th April 2007 magnussoft Deutschland GmbH announced that it stopped the distribution of magnussoft Zeta 1.21 and magnussoft Zeta 1.5 because of arisen uncertainty about the legal position:

"With immediate effect, magnussoft Deutschland GmbH has stopped the distribution of magnussoft Zeta 1.21 and magnussoft Zeta 1.5. According to the statement of Access Co. Ltd., neither yellowTAB GmbH nor magnussoft Deutschland GmbH are authorized to distribute Zeta.

This cessation is valid until the facts are clarified or reconfirmed.

We immediately approached our licenser for clarification of the legal position. Mr. Korz stated towards our lawyer that he would not be interested in cooperating with magnussoft Deutschland in this matter.

---

7 *Information gathered and combined from two sources:*
   Source 1: Haikuware: Website bebits.com,
         in the internet: http://wiki.bebits.com/page/BeOsReleases, Date: 23rd July 2010
   Source 2: Berka, Stefan (2004 to 2010): www.operating-system.org (last update of the page about BeOS: 2010-05-14): BeOS, in the internet:
   http://www.operating-system.org/betriebssystem/_german/bs-beos.htm, Date: 20th July 2010
8 *Berka, Stefan (2004 to 2010): Zeta, in the internet:*
   http://www.operating-system.org/betriebssystem/_english/bs-zeta.htm, (last update of the page about Zeta: 2010-05-14), Date: 20th July 2010

BlueEyedOS is an operating system that is inspired by BeOS. Unlike the original BeOS, BlueEyedOS is powered by a Linux kernel. Te project was founded by Guillaume Maillard on July of 2001. On 14th April 2003 the first demo boot CD was released.

However, there are no news since 26th June 2003 on the website. It seems that the project is discontinued or paused.[10]

OpenBeOS was founded as an open source project in the year 2001. Some years later, in 2004, it was renamed in Haiku. At the moment Haiku is the only considerable project that is still active and successfully develops an operating system that could be called a successor of BeOS.

Until now two Alpha Versions of Haiku Release 1 were released:

Release date	Release	Comments
September 2009	Haiku R1 Alpha 1	x86 32 bit computer platform
May 2010	Haiku R1 Alpha 2	x86 32 bit computer platform

Table 2: Releases of Haiku

There are four versions of the Haiku R1 Alpha 2. The user can choose between GCC2, GCC2Hybrid, GCC4 and GCC4Hybrid. The differences between the usage of the GCC versions are also one of the main differences between Haiku and BeOS. Further information about the differences between these two operating systems can be found on the following pages.

---

9 *Quotation: magnussoft Deutschland® GmbH (5th April 2007): Magnussoft cease distribution of Zeta, in the internet: http://www.zeta-os.com/cms/news.php?extend.50, Date: 20th July 2010*

10 *http://www.blueeyedos.com: BlueEyedOS, in the Internet: http://www.blueeyedos.com, Date: 20th July 2010*

1.2. Comparison between BeOS and Haiku

Haiku is more or less backward compatible with BeOS R5, but it is, except some source code for the Tracker and the Deskbar, not based on the BeOS source code:

"Haiku reimplements both the BeOS technologies as well as the end user experience, but it is far from being based on BeOS from a code base perspective. The only BeOS code that has made it into Haiku are Tracker and the Deskbar (the file manager and the equivalent of the start menu/taskbar, respectively). These were open sourced by Be Inc. back in 2001, later forked under the OpenTracker project, and eventually merged into the Haiku code base. The rest is either homebuilt code or derivatives of existing open source software."[11]

The goal of Haiku R1 is to recreate all important features of BeOS R5.
There are some ideas and plans for further development of Haiku. Further releases of Haiku, such as R2 and later, will perhaps have new features that are not available in BeOS R5.[12] Such ideas are discussed and documented in the project Glass Elevator: http://www.haiku-os.org/glass_elevator

However, there already exist some differences between BeOS R5 and Haiku R1, for example:[13]
- Haiku uses vector icons that are using a format implemented by Stippi.[14]
- One of the most popular web browsers for Haiku is WebPositive, a fast and small web browser that supports many modern features, such as tabbed browsing.
- Haiku supports many new hardware devices, which did not exist when BeOS R5 was developed. Haiku supports, among other devices, many modern LAN network cards by using drivers from the operating system FreeBSD. To make this possible, a layer is implemented. Furthermore, the support for WiFi devices is in development.
- Locale API is in development. It shall support the localization.
- The Layout API for Haiku is powerful in handling changes in text sizes and contents.[15]

---

11 *Quotation: Haiku, Inc.: General FAQ: Is Haiku based on BeOS then?, in the Internet: http://www.haiku-os.org/about/faq, Date: 24th July 2010*
12 *Thanks for the information to Alex von Gluck from the Haiku Community.*
13 *Thanks for some of the information to Truls Becken from the Haiku Community.*
14 *Stippi (Stippi): Why Haiku Vector Icons are So Small, article in: http://www.haiku-os.org/articles/2009-09-14_why_haiku_vector_icons_are_so_small, Date: 24th July 2010*
15 *Leavengood (2008-07-14): Laying It All Out, Part 1, article in: http://www.haiku-os.org/documents/dev/laying_it_all_out_part_1, Date: 24th July 2010*

- Haiku is open source. BeOS was a commercial operating system and closed source.
- Haiku is compiled with GCC2 or GCC4. There are also hybrid distributions of Haiku, such as Haiku GCC2Hybrid and GCC4Hybrid. BeOS was compiled with GCC2. Many modern computer games which are released for Haiku require GCC4 and additional libraries which also require GCC4, for example the SDL GCC4 Game Libraries (GETTEXT (libintl), SDL and SDL_MIXER).
- Until now Haiku runs only on x86 32 bit computer platforms. As already mentioned in the previous chapter, there exist BeOS versions for x86, PowerPC and BeBox. According to information on the website haiku-os.org, there are ports of Haiku to some other platform underway, for example for ARM, MIPS and PowerPC, but it is not clear whether they will be supported or not.[16]

---

16 *Haiku, Inc.: General FAQ: What platform(s) is Haiku targeted to run on?, in the Internet: http://www.haiku-os.org/about/faq, Date: 24th July 2010*

<u>**2. The architecture of Haiku**</u>

In this chapter the architecture and the most important modules of Haiku are shortly described. Readers, who are interested in further information, could take a look in the official documentations which can be found in the Haiku book: http://api.haiku-os.org/

2.1. Overview about the architecture

The architectures of operating systems can be classified in a few architecture types. The three most important architecture types are the microkernel, monolithic kernel and hybrid kernel:

- **Microkernel:**

  Operating systems that are based on a microkernel contain only a minimum or only a little bit more than the minimum amount of software in the kernel. The kernel contains software for core mechanisms such as the memory management, the thread and process management and inter-process-communication. All other parts of the operating systems, such as the application server, the file server, the drivers and many other components are outside of the kernel. The microkernel architecture can have advantages regarding the security because most parts of the operating systems are outside of the kernel and a virus infection of an application or a module does not always result in an infection of the kernel. If an application or device driver in the user mode crashes or freezes, it does not mean that the kernel crashes or freezes; the operating system may still be stable and can continue to work without a restart of the whole operating system. One of the disadvantages of operating systems based on microkernels is the lower performance: "In the monolithic system, the service is obtained by a single system call, which requires two mode switches (changes of the processor's privilege level). In the microkernel-based system, the service is obtained by sending an IPC message to a server, and obtaining the result in another IPC message from the server. This requires a context switch if the drivers are implemented as processes, or a function call if they are implemented as procedures. In addition, passing actual data to the server and back may incur extra copying overhead, while in a monolithic system the kernel can directly access the data in the client's buffers."[17]

  Examples of operating systems that are based on microkernel architecture are Symbian OS, QNX Neutrino, ChorusOS, MorphOS and Singularity.[18]

---

17 *Quotation: Wikipedia: http://en.wikipedia.org/wiki/Microkernel, Date: 24th July 2010*
18 *Wikipedia: http://de.wikipedia.org/wiki/Mikrokernel, Date: 25th July 2010*

- **Monolithic kernel:**

Operating systems that are based on the monolithic kernel architecture contain all or almost all software components and modules inside the kernel. The entire operating system runs in the kernel space with the permissions of the superuser mode. On the one hand, such operating systems are often faster than those that are based on the microkernel architecture. On the other hand, monolithic kernel based operating systems have more serious problems regarding the security than microkernel based operating systems. Examples of operating systems that are based on monolithic kernel architecture are Microsoft Windows 95, Microsoft Windows 98, Microsoft Windows 98SE, Windows Me, Microsoft DOS, Linux, Android and some Unix kernels such as FreeBSD, MacOSX, NetBSD, OpenBSD, SunOS, AIX and OpenSolaris.[19]

- **Hybrid kernel:**

The architecture of operating systems based on hybrid kernels is a combining of aspects of microkernels and monolithic kernels. In most cases the file server and the applications run in user mode, while the device drivers and the Application IPC run in kernel mode, although not all device drivers run in the kernel mode. The idea is to combine the advantages of both: the stability and security of the microkernel and the better performance of the monolith kernel. However, many people say that the term hybrid kernel is more or less only a marketing term. From the technical point of view, the two main types of architectures of operating systems are the microkernel and the monolithic kernel. The hybrid kernel is nothing really new, it is only a mix of these two main types of architectures. Examples of operating systems that are based on hybrid kernel architecture are many modern and popular operating systems, such as Microsoft Windows NT, Windows 2000, Windows Server 2003, Windows XP, Windows Vista, Windows Server 2008 and Windows 7.[20]

---

19 *Wikipedia: http://en.wikipedia.org/wiki/Monolithic_kernel, Date: 24th July 2010*
20 *Wikipedia: http://en.wikipedia.org/wiki/Hybrid_kernel, Date: 25th July 2010*

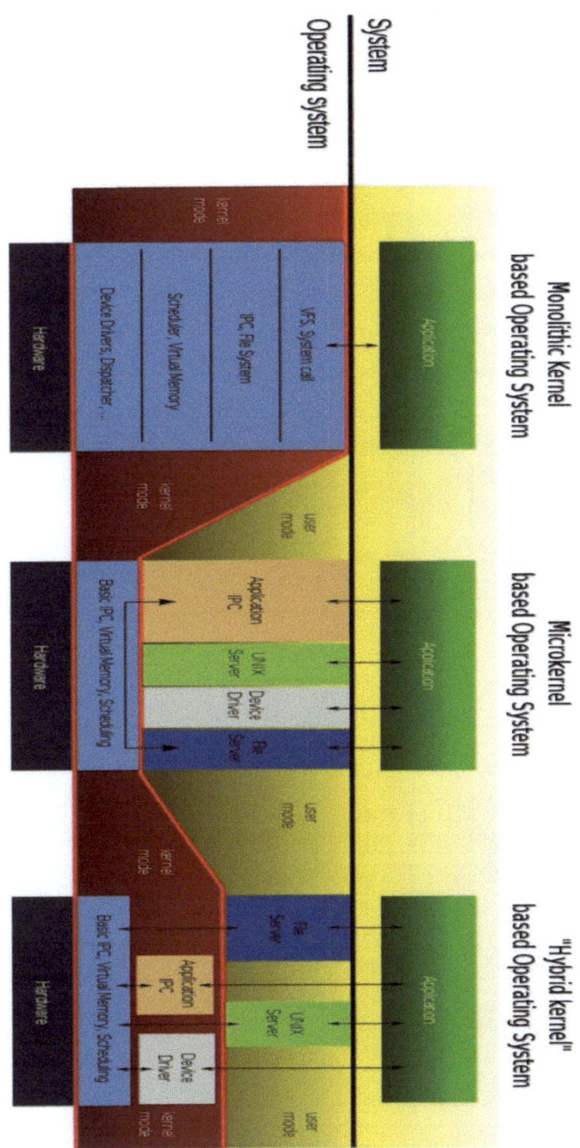

Graphic 1: Main types of kernels of operating systems[21]

---

21 *Golftheman: Monolith-, Micro- and a "hybrid" kernel, a draft of new version, This is a diagram from the Wikimedia Commons, 17th July 2008. Please note that I stretched the diagram. The original diagram has an other size proportion.*
In the internet: http://en.wikipedia.org/wiki/File:OS-structure2.svg

The operating systems BeOS and Haiku are based on the hybrid kernel architecture (see graphic 2). They try to combine the advantages of microkernels, which are safety and stability, with the advantages of the monolithic kernel architecture: high performance. As already mentioned, BeOS is also called the Multimedia OS. Therefore high performance is a very important aspect of this operating system.

In Haiku the nv_driver (the Nvidia graphic driver), the old BeOS drivers and some modules such as the Device Manager, Disk Device Manager, FS Layer, IPC, Memory Manager and Process Control run respectively are positioned in kernel mode. The servers, such as the Application Server, the Media Server and the Input Server run in the user mode. Furthermore, the kits (see next chapter), POSIX and the applications also run in the user mode. Please note that the light-orange box "Kernel" in the orange box "Kits" in the diagram is not the Kernel. The Kernel Kit is a part of the application programming interface of Haiku. Further information is available in the next chapter.

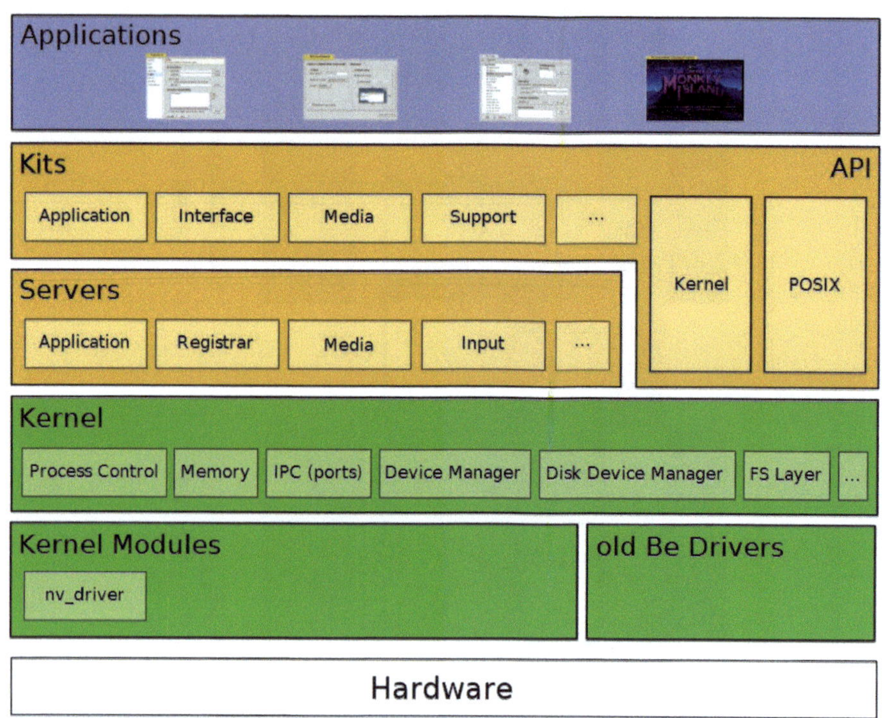

Graphic 2: Architecture of Haiku[22]

22 *Drinkwater, J. (2006): Haiku kernel diagram, in the internet: http://ezri.nextraweb.com,*
   Date: 11th August 2010

However, please note that Haiku is still in development and all information about the architecture, the kits and other technical aspects of Haiku are only a snapshot. At the moment I do not know how Haiku will look like when the official release 1 or further versions will be released. Various changes are possible.

2.2. Overview about the most important kits

From the point of view of application developers the kits in BeOS respectively Haiku are very important components of the operating system because they are the intermediate components between the applications and the core components of the kernel (see graphic 3).

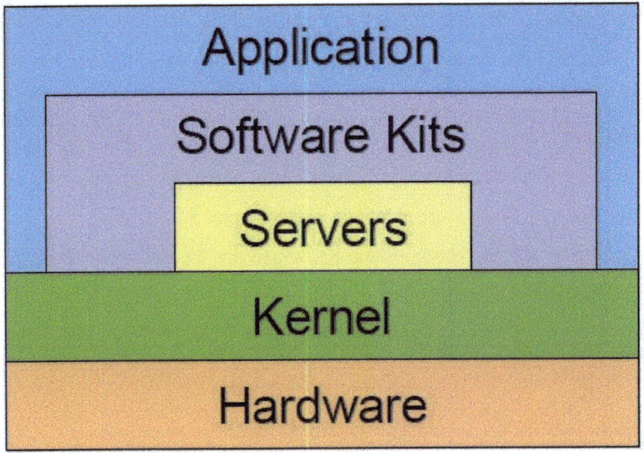

Graphic 3: Layers of Haiku[23]

Haiku respectively BeOS have several application programming interfaces, called kits, which will be shortly described in this chapter. However, it is not the goal of this thesis to give the developers detailed information about the kits. Readers who want to know more about the structure, classes and methods of the kits can take a look in the BeOS Bible and in the in official documentation of Haiku: http://api.haiku-os.org.
In this chapter you will get an overview about the all important kits.

____

23 *Yoder, J. (2010): Learning to program with Haiku, Lesson 15*

The application programming interface of Haiku is completely object oriented. The two most important kits are the Application Kit and the Interface Kit.

The Application Kit:

The classes of the Application Kit establish an application as an identifiable identity and gives them the possibilities to communicate and cooperate with other applications by using messaging. Each application has exactly one BApplication object which establishes a connection with the Application Server of BeOS and runs the main message loop of the application. This object is the representation of the application from the point of view of all other running applications. The Application Kit is also responsible for messaging (user event messages such as a mouse click, intraprocess and interprocess messaging). Furthermore, the Application Kit provides an interface to the clipboard (copy and paste functionalities) by using the BClipboard object and it keeps a track of all running applications (identification of the applications, starting the applications and get information to establish a communication with the applications) by using the class BRoster.[24]

The Interface Kit:

This kit contains a set of classes that are important for the interactive graphic user interface. Further information about the Interface Kit are available in the chapter 5.2.2.

Besides the Application Kit and the Interface Kit which are the two most important kits in BeOS respectively Haiku, there are many other important kits which will be shortly described on the following pages. The Game Kit plays an important role in fields of games development and will be described in the chapter 5.3.

The Device Kit:

This kit contains classes that could be used to access to hardware. Until now it contains only two classes: the BJoystick and the BSerial.

The BJoystick can be used as an interface to access a joystick or an other game controller.

The BSerial class contains methods that can be used to manage an RS-232 serial connection. Data can be received and written over the serial connection. A connection can be opened and closed. There are several methods in this class. Please read the documentations for further information about the BSerial methods.[25]

---

24 *The Be Development Team (1997): Be Developer's Guide, O'Reilly & Associates, p. 15 to 144*
25 *ACCESS Co., Ltd., Be Inc.: The Be Book - System Overview - The Device Kit, in the internet: http://www.haiku-os.org/legacy-docs/bebook/TheDeviceKit_Overview.html, Date: 10th August 2010*

The Game Kit:

Further information about the Game Kit are available in the chapter 5.3.

The Input Server:

This system service receives user events, mostly mouse or keyboard events, and dispatches them to the application server. The Input Server can load add-ons that filter and modify the input events. There are various types of add-ons. For example, one type of add-ons can convert keyboard input in character sets that can be entered with a standard keyboard only by using a combination of many keys, such as the Japanese Kanji characters.[26]

The Kernel Kit:

This kit contains a set of C functions which are used to set and control the context in which an application runs. Among other things, the functions in the Kernel Kit are used to protect the code and data of pieces of software and to synchronise the execution of two or more threads, for example by using semaphores.[27]

The Mail Kit:

This kit contains services that are used for electronic mails in the internet. Among other things, the Mail Kit provides mechanisms that are useful for:

- The configuration of mail accounts of the users.
- Receiving electronic mails by using the POP (Post Office Protocol).
- Sending electronic mails by using the SMTP (Simple Mail Transfer Protocol).
- The configuration of the electronic mail daemon.[28]

---

26 *ACCESS Co., Ltd., Be Inc.: The Be Book - System Overview - The Input Server, in the internet: http://www.haiku-os.org/legacy-docs/bebook/TheInputServer_Overview.html, Date: 25th July 2010*

27 *The Be Development Team (1997): Be Developer's Guide, O'Reilly & Associates, p. 731 to 804*

28 *ACCESS Co., Ltd., Be Inc.: The Be Book - System Overview - The Mail Kit, in the internet: http://www.haiku-os.org/legacy-docs/bebook/TheMailKit_Overview_Introduction.html, Date: 25th July 2010*

The Media Kit:

The media kit is a very important part of Haiku and BeOS. As mentioned before, BeOS was called the Multimedia OS. One reason for this is the powerful media kit. It supports many types of media, especially audio and video. Playback and recording is supported for various devices.[29]

The Midi Kit:

This kit provides features that enable the developer to use MIDI (Musical Instrument Digital Interface) that is a standard for music data.

The Be Book says:

"...The Midi Kit understands the MIDI software format (including Standard MIDI Files). With the Kit, you can create a network of objects that generate and broadcast MIDI messages. Applications built with the Midi Kit can read MIDI data that's brought into the computer through a MIDI port, process the data, write it to a file, and send it back out through the same port. The Kit also contains a General MIDI synthesizer that you can use to realize your MIDI scores. This is a software synthesizer that includes reverberation..."[30]

The Network Kit:

This kit contains some classes which are used for network programming. For example, the class BNetAddress can be used to construct network addresses and convert them into other formats.[31]

The OpenGL Kit:

This kit contains only the class BGLView which enables the developer to display graphics that are rendered by using the OpenGL graphics library. The OpenGL library is useful to create 3D graphics in games and applications.[32]

---

29 *ACCESS Co., Ltd., Be Inc.: The Be Book - System Overview - The Media Kit, in the internet:*
   http://www.haiku-os.org/legacy-docs/bebook/TheMediaKit_Overview.html,
   Date: 14th October 2010
30 *Quotation: ACCESS Co., Ltd., Be Inc.: The Be Book - System Overview - The Midi Kit, in the*
   internet:
   http://www.haiku-os.org/legacy-docs/bebook/TheMidiKit_Introduction.html,
   Date: 14th October 2010
31 *ACCESS Co., Ltd., Be Inc.: The Be Book - System Overview - The Network Kit, in the internet:*
   http://www.haiku-os.org/legacy-docs/bebook/TheNetworkKit_Overview.html,
   Date: 25th July 2010
32 *ACCESS Co., Ltd., Be Inc.: The Be Book - System Overview - The OpenGL Kit, in the internet:*
   http://www.haiku-os.org/legacy-docs/bebook/TheOpenGLKit_Overview.html,
   Date: 14th October 2010

The Storage Kit:

This kit contains C functions and C++ classes that are used to work with the file system. Among many other things, it allows you to:

- Access files, read and write them.
- Detect changes of files.
- Navigate in the folders.
- Read and change the attributes of nodes.
- Search files by using their name or meta data.[33]

The Support Kit:

This kit contains classes that can be used by any application, not depending on the type and purpose of the application. Many of these classes provide methods that are very useful for the daily work of programmers, for example debugging tools, error codes for all software kits, protocols for objects, mechanisms for locking, standard constants and data types and containers for data items.[34]

The Translation Kit:

Although the name of this kit may let you think that it could be used to support the developer in fields of localisation of applications, this kit has a very different purpose. It is responsible for converting data streams between various, more or less different data formats.

In the Be Book this very intelligibly example was given:

"A word processor, for example, could use the Translation Kit to import and export documents in a variety of formats, including HTML, PostScript, and plain ASCII, while working in its own native format."[35]

---

33 *The Be Development Team (1997): Be Developer's Guide, O'Reilly & Associates, p. 149 to 321*
34 *The Be Development Team (1997): Be Developer's Guide, O'Reilly & Associates, p. 807 to 850*
35 *ACCESS Co., Ltd., Be Inc.: The Be Book - System Overview - The Translation Kit,*
  in the internet:
  http://www.haiku-os.org/legacy-docs/bebook/TheTranslationKit_Introduction.html,
  Date: 25th July 2010

3. The file system of Haiku

In this chapter we will take a look at the file system of BeOS. The Be File System (BFS) is the native file system of BeOS. Some of the most important features and characteristics of the Be File System are:

- The BFS uses i-nodes. The extended file attributes are stored in the i-node.
- It is a 64 bit file system. The theoretical maximum size of a file is around 18 000 petabytes, but it is very unlikely than such big hard disks will be available within the next several years. As already mentioned, BeOS is also called the Multimedia Operating System. Multimedia files, such as high quality audio and video files, can be very big. Therefore the support of very big files is one important aspect of the Be File System. Further information and thoughts about this topic are available in the chapter 4.1.
- It supports journaling. A system journal is used to track all transaction to the disk. This ensures a better data integrity. Furthermore, the state of the system, including all variables and even the positions of the windows in the graphic user interface, is safe and can be restored in case of a system crash. The boot times after a crash are almost as short as after a normal restart because all the necessary data is available in the journal.
- The BFS is a file system that supports the hierarchical structure of files and folders.
- Extended file attributes are supported, such as meta data of files. This makes advanced search options possible. The search possibilities are more or less similar to the searches in a relational data base by using queries. Further information and thoughts about this topic are available in the chapter 5.2.1.
- Multithreaded access to the disk is supported. The goal is to realize an optimum disk performance even when two or more tasks access to the disk at the same time.

Haiku uses OpenBFS which is mainly a reimplementation of the Be File System. OpenBFS is not only the native file system of Haiku, it is also known to the developers of the operating system SkyOS because the file system SkyFS is based on OpenBFS.[36]

In the book Practical File System Design with the Be File System from Dominic Giampaolo, Be Inc., some benchmarks and corresponding results are described.

According to his conclusions, on the one hand the BFS performs very well in writing and reading

---

36 *Hacker, S. / Bortman, H. / Herborth, C. (1999): The BeOS Bible, Peachpit Press, California, pages 11 to 14.*

big files of streaming data. The BFS achieved about 99 percentage of the available bandwidth of the hard disk drive because the overhead of the input and output process was very small. Furthermore, the Be File system is fast in updating the meta data of files when the size of the data is small enough to fit in the cache.

On the other hand, the Be File System is slow when modifying large amounts of data that are stored in many small files. According to Dominic Giampaolo the problems are the lack of a unified virtual memory and buffer cache system. Furthermore, he wrote that the indexing, which is by default active in the Be File System, decreases the performance on meta data update benchmarks. When the indexing is deactivated, the performance on meta data update benchmarks is about doubled, in some cases it is even more than doubled.[37]

Detailed benchmark results are available in the book Practical File System Design with the Be File System from Dominic Giampaolo. However, they will not be discussed in this thesis because the used hardware and operating systems in the benchmarks are old and the Be File System is not a main part of this thesis. The purpose of this chapter was to give the reader a short overview about the most important features of the Be File System.

As you can see, the Be File System has been supporting many modern features since the 1990s. Some of these features are not available even in the file systems of modern, commercial operating systems. Furthermore, the Be File System is very fast in reading and writing large streaming media data files, for example high quality video and audio files. This is one of many reasons why BeOS is called the Multimedia Operating System.

---

37 *Giampaolo, D. (1999): Practical File System Design with the Be File System, Morgan Kaufmann Publishers, INC., California, pages 139 to 150.*

4. Objectives and market positioning

In this chapter the specific features of BeOS and Haiku are described. Furthermore, the objectives and the possible market potential of Haiku will be discussed.

In the chapters 5 and 6 some of these objectives and potential market positioning will be checked by analysing the capabilities for multimedia and games (see chapter 5) and the behaviour and expectations of the Haiku community (see chapter 6).

Haiku is inspired by on BeOS which is called the Multimedia Operating system because it had many modern and innovative features already in the 1990s when most private computer users had the operating systems Microsoft DOS, Microsoft Windows 3.1, Microsoft Windows 95 or Microsoft Windows 98. In the first half of the 1990s decade most computer games ran with Microsoft DOS or they ran with other hardware platforms, such as the Amiga, a home computer that was popular because of the advanced features in fields of multimedia and the low prices. Windows 3.1 was not popular among developers of computer games because this operating system had no advanced and fast libraries for 3D graphics and it needed much memory that was expensive in the 1990s. Therefore most PC games ran with Microsoft DOS which did not need much memory, so most of it was available for the games.

In the second part of the 1990s decade Windows became popular for computer games because Microsoft introduced Microsoft DirectX for Windows 95 and Windows 98. DirectX is a runtime environment that is used by many computer games nowadays. It supports many features that are very important for the developers of computer games, such as 2D and 3D graphic programming (DirectDraw and Direct3D), MIDI music playback (DirectMusic), sound playback (DirectSound), usage of input devices such as the keyboard and joysticks (DirectInput) and network capabilities for multi player computer games (DirectPlay).

However, Windows 95 and Windows 98 were still not really powerful in fields of multimedia and games. Both operating systems supported a 32 bit file system (FAT 32) and had a maximum file size limit of about 4 GB. This was a problem for some people who recorded and edited big audio or video files. Such files needed much disk space, especially if they were not compressed or used only low compression rates. Such file formats with no or only low compression rates were used by many video and audio editing applications because the high compressed files were not editable or there were compatibility or performance problems. After the editing, they were compressed with codecs that offered high compression rates and used for playback.

Therefore many people who worked with tools for audio and video editing had problems because of the 4 GB file size limit of the FAT32. BeOS has the Be File System, a 64 bit file system, that supports a maximum file size of around 18 000 petabytes. This was and is still much more than any video or audio editing software needs. Even the modern Dual-Layer Blue-Ray discs for high definitions movies have a capacity of only about 50 GB. Of course, in most cases movies on such discs are compressed, but even the uncompressed formats would have a size of a few hundreds of gigabytes, maybe a few or several terabytes, but this would be a lot less than 18 000 petabytes. Please note that one petabyte is about one thousand terabytes (1000 or 1024 terabytes, it depends on the definition and the field of usage).

Furthermore, Microsoft Windows 95 and Windows 98 supported only a single central processing unit. BeOS supported up to eight processors. This was also an important feature for multimedia because it was possible to run two tasks simultaneously, for example the encoding of audio and video data by using two different codec algorithms.

Because of these and some other reasons, such as the focus on a user friendly graphic user interface and some similarities with Amiga OS and Apple Mac OS, BeOS was called the Multimedia Operating system. Even today there are relatively many multimedia applications for BeOS and Haiku. On haikuware.com, one of the biggest website about software for Haiku and BeOS, the two biggest categories of software are games and multimedia: there are 418 entries listed in the category games and 398 applications are listed in the category multimedia. For detailed information please take a look at this list:

Category	Number of entries
Games	418
Multimedia	398
Utilities	384
Development	373
Internet and network	319
Drivers	214
System files	140
Info management	96
Emulators	92

Entertainment	84
Productivity	63
Geek toys	46
Science and math	34

Table 3: Categories of software on haikuware.com[38]

However, nowadays Microsoft Windows XP and newer versions of Windows are powerful operating systems in fields of multimedia and games, especially because of the DirectX runtime and the support of multi core processors. Furthermore, newer versions of Windows support file sizes up to about 16 terabyte by using the New Technology File System (NTFS). Of course, 16 terabytes are a lot less than the 18 000 petabytes which are possible by using the Be File System, but most users do not need such big files at the moment because most hard disks in personal computers have a capacity of less than 16 terabytes. However, this could change when hard disks become much bigger and cheaper in future.

Is Haiku the Multimedia Operating System nowadays?

From my point of view, it is not the Multimedia Operating System at the moment because up-to-date drivers for many modern graphic cards are not available. Without these drivers the operating system can not use the maximum power and all the features of modern graphic cards which play an important role in 3D computer games and the rendering of 3D objects and worlds. Furthermore, the up-to-date versions of some widely used multimedia technologies such as the Adobe Flash Player are not available for Haiku.

Nevertheless, Haiku is powerful in fields of multimedia and if it becomes more popular, then the developers and producers of modern multimedia technology and drivers for modern graphic cards may have a motivation to create releases of their software for Haiku, too. In the chapter 5.3 the capabilities of Haiku in fields of multimedia and computer games will be described and discussed.

Although Haiku is perhaps not the Multimedia Operating System nowadays, it is still a very user friendly and fast Desktop Operating System. In the chapters 5.1 respectively 5.2 further information about some aspects of a user friendly operating system in general respectively the implementation of these aspects in Haiku are available.

---

38 *Haikuware: File repository for Haiku and BeOS software,*
in the internet: haikuware.com, Date: 31st July 2010

What are possible market positions of Haiku?

It is very difficult to answer this question at the moment. Haiku is still in development. At the moment the newest version is Haiku Alpha 2 which is quite powerful, but it is still only an alpha version. Furthermore, as already mentioned, the goal of the Release 1 is to reimplement most of the features of BeOS Release 5. Although BeOS was a very advanced and innovative operating system in the 1990s and some of the features are still not available in competitors such as Microsoft Windows or Linux, BeOS is old and no leader in fields of multimedia any more.

Therefore Haiku has to be better and more advanced than BeOS to become a leader in fields of multimedia. Whether it will be able to improve depends on the ideas and implementations in the Release 2 and later.

However, from my point of view it may become popular in an other field, too. Haiku is very user friendly and it has very low hardware requirements. Therefore it could be interesting for users who simply want to have a fast and user friendly desktop operating system that can be used for the common tasks such as listening to music, watching movies, writing letters, browsing in the internet and playing some casual games. Perhaps Haiku could be able to meet the requirements of such users already in the first stable release that will be perhaps available within the next two years. There are several reasons why Haiku could become a popular desktop operating operating system.

Firstly, Haiku has a focus on the graphic user interface. Unlike Linux, where the graphic user interface is just some kind of an add-on, the graphic user interface is one of the main and essential parts of Haiku. It is not possible to boot or work without the graphic user interface. The graphic user interface is optimized regarding both aspects: performance and usability.

In the chapter 5.2 further information is available.

Secondly, Haiku is very fast, especially regarding the boot time. The booting speed was also one of the advantages of BeOS which was also very fast. Here are some benchmarks that I made with my personal computer and my notebook.

Please note that this benchmarks are not very accurate because in all cases the operating system Haiku is installed on a hard disk together with other operating systems. Therefore the position of the Haiku partition on the hard disk is probably neither at the beginning nor at the end of the physical hard disk. The position on the hard disk could influence the boot speed because the rotation speed of the hard disk has effects on the read and write speed, depending on the positions of the partition.

The benchmarking was manually done by using a clock and eyes. I started the clock when I started Haiku from the operating system boot menu and stopped the clock as soon as the desktop was totally built up, including all icons, and the mouse could be freely moved. In general I noticed that this means that the booting is over or almost over because I could start the Web Positive web browser within a few seconds and the hard disk seems not to be very busy. Although the above mentioned methods and circumstances can not ensure accurate benchmark results, they may be used to determine the order of magnitude of the boot speed.

System	Boot time in seconds
Benchmark 1: Haiku R1 Alpha 2 GCC2 Hybrid Revision 36769, Kernel 8th May 2010, PC with AMD Phenom II X4 3.4 GHz (overclocked), Gigabyte GA-MA790XT-UD4P mainboard, 4 GB DDR3 1333 RAM, 250 GB 3.5" 7200 rps hard disk WDC WD5000AAKS SATA, Nvidia GeForce 9500 GT graphic card with 512 MB video memory	10
Benchmark 2: Haiku R1 Alpha 2 GCC2 Hybrid Revision 36769, Kernel 8th May 2010, PC with AMD Phenom II X4 3.2 GHz, Gigabyte GA-MA790XT-UD4P mainboard, 4 GB DDR3 1333 RAM, 250 GB 3.5" 7200 rps hard disk WDC WD5000AAKS SATA, Nvidia GeForce 9500 GT graphic card with 512 MB video memory	10
Benchmark 3: Haiku R1 Alpha 2 GCC2 Hybrid Revision 36769, Kernel 8th May 2010, PC with AMD Phenom II X4 1.0 GHz, 4 GB DDR3 1333 RAM, 250 GB 3.5" 7200 rps hard disk WDC WD5000AAKS SATA, Nvidia GeForce 9500 GT graphic card with 512 MB video memory	12
Benchmark 4: Nightly build Haiku R1 Alpha 2 GCC2 Hybrid Revision 37453, Kernel 10th July 2010, PC with AMD Sempron 3000 clocked at 2.0 GHz, ASUS A7V8X mainboard, 1 GB DDR RAM 333 MHz, 80 GB 3.5" 7200 rpm hard disk IMB/HITACHI IC35L080AVVA07-0 IDE, Nvidia GeForce 7600 GS graphic card with 258 MB video memory	17
Benchmark 5: Nightly build Haiku R1 Alpha 2 GCC2 Hybrid Revision 37453 Kernel 10th July 2010 PC with AMD Sempron 3000 clocked at 1.2 GHz, ASUS A7V8X mainboard, 1 GB DDR RAM 333 MHz, 80 GB 3.5" 7200 rpm hard disk IMB/HITACHI IC35L080AVVA07-0 IDE, Nvidia GeForce 7600 GS graphic card with 258 MB video memory	18

Benchmark 6: Nightly build Haiku R1 Alpha 2 GCC2 Hybrid Revision 37453, Kernel 10th July 2010, Notebook with Intel Core Duo 1.73 GHz with only one core enabled, 2 GB RAM PC2 5300S, 160 GB 2.5" 5400 rps hard disk Fujitsu MHW2160BH PL ATA, ATI Radeon XPRESS 1250, CPU Power Saving Mode disabled, Intel Step Speed disabled	20
Benchmark 7: Ubuntu 20.10 Maverick Meerkat x86 32 Bit, PC with AMD Phenom II X4 3.2 GHz, Gigabyte GA-MA790XT-UD4P mainboard, 4 GB DDR3 1333 RAM, 250 GB 3.5" 7200 rps hard disk WDC WD5000AAKS SATA, Nvidia GeForce 9500 GT graphic card with 512 MB video memory	17
Benchmark 8: PC BSD 8.1 x86 32 Bit, Kernel 8th May 2010, PC with AMD Phenom II X4 3.2 GHz, Gigabyte GA-MA790XT-UD4P mainboard, 4 GB DDR3 1333 RAM, 250 GB 3.5" 7200 rps hard disk WDC WD5000AAKS SATA, Nvidia GeForce 9500 GT graphic card with 512 MB video memory	75

Table 4: Benchmark of the booting speed of Haiku

Please note that I had to disable the second CPU core in the notebook because when both are enabled, the Haiku operating system can not boot. This seems to be a compatibility problem since the version Haiku Release 1 Alpha 2. The version Haiku Release 1 Alpha 1 works with both CPU cores without any noticeable boot problems.

Furthermore, please note that I used two versions of Haiku: the official Haiku R1 Alpha 2 GCC2 Hybrid Revision 36769 and the nightly build Haiku R1 Alpha 2 GCC2 Hybrid Revision 37453. The official Haiku R1 Alpha 2 version has some installation problems that are well known to the developers and the Haiku community. Therefore a nightly build had been used to avoid the problems in some of the systems. However, there are probably no noticeable differences in the booting speeds between these versions.

As you can see the performance of the boot speed depends very much on the speed of the hard disk. Although the CPU frequency of the AMD Phenom II X4 was decreased from 3.2 GHz to 1.0 GHz, there was only a small effect on the boot speed: the boot time increased from about 10 to about 12 seconds. There was also no big difference between the boot speed results when decreasing the CPU clock of an AMD Sempron 3000 from 2.0 GHz to 1.2 GHz. However, the notebook is much slower regarding the boot speed because the 2.5" hard disk is much slower.

In general, the boot speed of Haiku is amazing, especially if you consider that Haiku boots and starts a graphic user interface and not a simple command line bash console. Consider that latest versions of Windows and most Linux distributions with a graphical user interface need much more time to boot than Haiku. This is proven by the benchmarks 2, 7 and 8 that were processed with exactly the same hardware and even by using the same hard disk partition. Haiku (10 seconds) boots much faster than Ubuntu Linux (17 seconds) and PC BSD (75 seconds).

Thirdly, Haiku has very low system requirements. According to the website haiku-os.org, the version Haiku Alpha 2 requires only 128 MB memory. It has been tested to work on a CPU as slow as a Pentium II 400 MHz and requires about 700 MB disk space.[39]

Finally, Haiku is free to use. Most parts of Haiku are released under the MIT license.[40]
When we consider that Haiku is free to use and it requires only an entry level computer, then it could be possible to produce a computer equipped with Haiku for less than 200 Euro. Such a computer could be used for common daily tasks such as writing e-mails and letters, reading PDF documents, listening to music, browsing in the web and watching movies. Additionally, the user could even do small video and audio editing tasks and play some 2D and simple 3D games. The booting would be fast, even when using entry level PCs or notebooks.

Therefore my thesis is that Haiku could become a popular, user-friendly and fast operating system that has only low hardware requirements and can be used in cheap PCs, notebooks and netbooks.
On long term, perhaps it will become a powerful multimedia operating system, too. But this depends not only on the Haiku community, but also on the the developers and producers of hardware devices and multimedia technologies, such as Nvidia, ATI, Adobe and many others. It depends on whether they will release up-to-date drivers and software components for Haiku or not.

---

39 *Haiku, Inc.: Release Notes, Haiku R1 Alpha 2, in the Internet:*
   http://www.haiku-os.org/get-haiku/release-notes, Date: 31st July 2010
40 *Haiku, Inc.: General FAQ, What license is Haiku released under?, in the Internet:*
   http://www.haiku-os.org/about/faq, Date: 31st July 2010

<u>**5. The user-friendliness and multimedia capabilities of Haiku**</u>

This is one of the main chapters of this thesis. The goals are to analyse the graphic user interface with focus on the user-friendliness (see chapter 5.2) and the capabilities for multimedia applications and games (see chapter 5.3). But first of all, some general aspects of software ergonomics with focus on software with visual display terminals and graphic user interfaces shall be described.

5.1. General aspects of software ergonomics

The International Organisation for Standardization, also called ISO, explains in ISO 9241-11 the ergonomic requirements for office work with visual display terminals. It explains that a software is not in general good or bad, but the requirements depend on the context of use of the software. The goal is to describe the usability of a software which depends on the efficiency, effectiveness and satisfaction of the user.

The effectiveness describes whether a software enables the user to successfully do his tasks and get correct results. For example, a word processing application should be able to correctly print a document and the integrated grammar check should be able to correctly check the grammar, at least the most important aspects.

The efficiency describes how much time and brainpower the user must invest to do his job by using the software. A good software should help the user to do his job much faster and with less cognitive load and problems than without the software.

The satisfaction of the user describes how much the user likes to use the software to complete his tasks by using the software. This depends among other things on the subjective satisfaction of the user and his opinion about the software.

A very important part of the ergonomic requirements of software with visual display terminals are the dialogue principles. In the ISO 9241-10 these seven principles are described:[41]

---

41 *Böhle, F.: Softwareentwicklung als Arbeits- und Organisationsgestaltung – Softwareergonomie,*
Extraordinat für Sozioökonomie der Arbeits- und Berufswelt, WiSo Fakultät, Universität
Augsburg, chapter I.1, year is unknown, perhaps about 2000. (GERMAN)

- **Suitability for the task:**

  The software should offer information and functions to the user that support him by completing his tasks. The software should support the user to complete his specific tasks without disturbing and confusing him by other functions that may cause problems.

- **Suitability for the learning:**

  The software should help the user to learn how to work with the software and how to navigate in the dialogues. New users should be enabled to fast learn to work with the software. For example, this could be realised by offering high quality documentation, tutorials and tool tips.

- **Transparency and self-descriptiveness:**

  The dialogues should be easy to understand or contain descriptions and instructions that can be accessed by the user. The user should be able to understand how the dialogue works and why it works the way it is.

- **Conformity with user expectations:**

  The dialogues shall contain elements and associated actions that are conform with the user expectations. The expectations of the user are based on his education, working experiences and general experiences. Furthermore, it is very important that the terms and symbols used in the software are consistent. A specific term or symbol in one dialogue shall have the same meaning in an other dialogue of the software.

- **Controllability:**

  The user should have the opportunity to control the speed and direction of navigation of a dialogue. Furthermore, he shall be able to control the order and amount of data that is read, written or displayed by the software.

- **Error tolerance:**

  This principle means that it is important that there are no fatal consequences if the user makes an error. The user shall have the opportunity to easily detect the error and to make corrections. For example, the software should contain field validators that check the syntax and the data type of the typed in data. If a field required a date that shall be entered by the user, then the software shall be able to detect, whether the entered data is a valid date and, in case of an invalid date, inform the user about the problem and give him the opportunity to enter a valid date.

- **Suitability for individualization:**

  The user shall have the opportunity to customize the software. For example, the user should be able to change the family and size of the fonts or to select the colours of the text, the screen or some other parts of the software.

Besides the above described principles there are also some other aspects that play an important role in fields of software ergonomics. One of them is the feedback. The software should give fast and useful feedbacks. For example, if the user clicks on a button to get data from a data base, then he would like to know whether the software is processing his request and if so, how long it may take until he will get the results. In this case the software should give feedback. For example, the feedback could be that the mouse pointer turns into a sand clock and a progress bar appears that displays the estimated elapsed and remaining times of the process.

An other important aspect is the respond time of the software, especially when interactive graphic user interfaces are used. According to the authors of the book *Readings in Information Visualization: Using Vision to Think*[42] there exist three levels of interaction depending on the speed of the response.

The **psychological moment** is located within about 0.1 seconds. Any events that happen within 0.1 seconds seems to belong together and are fused to one awareness.[43] This is important for animations and fast user interactions. If we press a button or move a slider and the displayed data is updated within 0.1 seconds, then we have the feeling that our action directly and immediately causes effects.

The **unprepared response** is located at about one second. This is a very important level for interactive dialogues because any response that needs more time than about one second seems to be slow and may let the user think that there may be some problems. In general a user is not prepared for any events that happen within one second. Therefore this level is called the unprepared response. Of course, the user will notice that the response needs some time, but it is fast enough to allow a fast user interaction and a work flow without any serious lags.

The average duration of a **unit task** is about ten seconds, but it can be between about five and thirty seconds. Within this time the user completes a common task, such as selecting an option in a menu or formatting a paragraph in a text document.

---

42 *Card K, S. / Mackinlay D., J. / Shneiderman, B. (1999): Readings in Information Visualization: Using Vision to Think, Academic Press, California, pages 231 et sequentes.*
43 *Please note that movies should have a much higher frame rate to look smooth. Most smooth movies run with at least about 25 frames per second. The psychological moment of about 0.1 seconds, which is equivalent to about 10 frames per second, is meant to be a theoretical level regarding the response speed in interactive dialogues. It is not meant to be used for computer games or movies.*

The faster the responses, the smoother seems to be the software from the subjective point of view of the user. Therefore Haiku is optimized for fast user interaction by fast displaying and updating elements and menus of the graphic user interface. This and other features of Haiku will be described in the next chapter.

From the point of view of the **cognitivism** an important aspect is the way how to display data and information on the desktop, the menus and the dialogues of a graphic user interface. An interesting theory is the **cognitive load theory** which is discussed in fields of learning and e-learning. This theory is very interesting because the graphic user interface of Haiku was developed intentionally or at random by taking some of the aspects and recommendations of the cognitive load theory into account. Therefore this theory will be explained here.

The Cognitive Load Theory describes the processes and structures of learning by taking into account that the human brain is limited regarding the memory capacities and speed of processing. There are three types of memories that humans use:

- The **sensory memory**:

  This is the first level memory. It works automatically and very fast without the awareness of the humans. The capacity of this memory is less than the capacity of the long-term memory, but greater than of the capacity of the working memory. The sensory memory is a very short-term memory. Data is lost after milliseconds or maybe a few seconds, depending on the organ of perception (eyes, hears, nose etc.). Between the sensory memory and the working memory there are some filters. Only a small part of the data is passed through the filter to the working memory. Let us take an example to understand it. Imagine that you are playing a computer game and you are a pilot that is fighting in the sky against evil aliens that are attacking you with their space ships. While flying in the sky your eyes will see many things, such as clouds, trees on the ground, flying birds and many other things. You also see the cockpit, the dust on your seat, the scratches on your joystick and many other things. While you are playing, you are sitting at home in your seat. There is a cup of tea on the table next to you, there are greeting cards that you got some days ago from a friend of you, there are plants near the window, there are hundreds of small or medium size things in your room. Although your yes see all these things, you will not be aware of most of these things. Your mind will set a focus on the enemies in their space ships and on the weapons that are opening fire. All the other things will not be within your awareness. They will not pass the filters between your sensory memory and the working memory. However, if suddenly an unexpected strong stimulus occurs, for example your cup of tea falls on the ground and the cup breaks into many pieces by creating a loud sound, then you will become aware of the cup of tea. As you can see, mostly important things with a strong stimulus pass the filter between your sensory memory and the working memory.

- The **working memory**:

This is the second level memory. It has a capacity of between about two and ten elements. The humans are aware of this memory and the elements in the capacity of this memory. The working memory is a fast memory regarding reading and writing. The data is stored for a short period, mostly the data gets lost after between about a few and thirty seconds. The data can be saved for long-term by copying it to the long-term memory. The working memory is the memory which you use to analyse new data and transform it. For example, think about mathematics. You have a new formula in a book and a few values that you want to put into the formula to calculate the result. The values and the formula are stored in your working memory while you are doing the calculations. In most cases you will forget the values after some seconds or a few minutes because the values were just examples to practice the usage of the formula. But perhaps the formula is useful and you will decide to memorize it for the future. If you decide so, you will concentrate and repeat the formula several times until it is copied into your long-term memory. Repeating and concentration are methods that can copy elements from the small working memory into the big long-term memory.

- The **long-term memory**:

This memory consists of semantic networks. The capacity is very large, but the writing is very slow. Read accesses are faster than the write accesses, but even the read accesses are slower than in case of the working memory. You are not directly aware of the elements in your long-term memory, but you can intentionally copy them into the working memory and make them ready for fast and direct access within your awareness.[44]

Besides the classification of the types of memory, there is also a classification of the types of loads in the cognitive load theory. There are three types of cognitive loads:[45]

- The **intrinsic load**:

This load is relevant to the learning and it depends on the learn contents. The intrinsic load depends on the complexity of the elements of the learning content and our prior knowledge.

---

44 *Tücke, Manfred (2003): Grundlagen der Psychologie für (zukünftige) Lehrer, pages 160 to 179, LIT Verlag Münster (GERMAN)*
45 *Rey, G. D.: E-Learning, Cognitive Load Theory, in the internet: http://www.elearning-psychologie.de/clt.html, Date: 26th June 2010, (GERMAN)*

The intrinsic load can not be influenced by the (visual) presentation of the learn contents. For example, there is no difference whether we use colours or only black and white text.

- The **extraneous** load:

  This load is not relevant to the learning. It depends on the (in most cases visual) presentation of the learn contents. The extraneous load does not depend on the learn contents. Therefore this type of load is the one that shall be decreased from the point of view of the cognitive load theory.

- The **germane** load:

  This load is relevant to the learning and depends among other things also on the presentation of the learn contents. The goal of the germane load is to understand the learn contents, to construct cognitive structures and to save the information and knowledge in the long-term memory. From the point of view of the cognitive load theory, the germane load shall be increased.

According to the cognitive load theory the goal is to increase or maximize the learning efficiency. The human shall be enabled to faster and easier understand the information, transform it, build up knowledge and save it in the long-term memory. This can be realized by optimizing the total cognitive load which consists of the three types of loads that were described above. The total cognitive load can be optimized by increasing or maximizing the types of loads that are relevant to the learning and decreasing or minimizing the type of load which is not relevant to the learning.

As already mentioned before, the intrinsic load depends on the learn contents. Therefore the only way to reduce it would mean to reduce the learn content, but this is often not the intention of the learner. Furthermore, if we would reduce the intrinsic load, then the total load would decrease, but we would not learn much and the learning efficiency would not be good. From the point of view of the cognitive load theory, the intrinsic load is often more or less a constant because the learner knows what he or she wants or has to learn.

The germane load shall be increased. By doing this the learner learns faster and more efficient.

But how can this be done?

The answer sounds very simple: the extraneous load should be reduced or minimized because this load is not relevant to the learning. Furthermore, it is quite easy to reduce the extraneous load because it depends on the (mostly visual) presentation. Therefore the cognitive load theory recommends regarding the presentation, for example:

- Do not use unnecessary special effects.

- Do not use too many colours.

- Multimedia content shall look simple.

- Avoid redundant repeating.

- Avoid animations or use them only rarely in Power Point screens.

- Important information should be clearly presented.

- Keep it simple.

- Less is more.

5.2. The graphic user interface

In this chapter the graphic user interface of Haiku will be analysed. Hereby both aspects will be taken into account: the psychological and general aspects of software ergonomics and the technical implementation of the graphic user interface in Haiku.

As already explained in the previous chapters, BeOS and Haiku are user-friendly operating systems with a focus on multimedia.

BeOS was inspired by some other operating systems, such as AmigaOS and MacOS. Both systems have a graphic user interface and count among the pioneers of user-friendly and powerful multimedia operating systems.

BeOS was popular among users who were interested in video and sound editing. Such users appreciate a fast and user-friendly graphic user interface. Therefore the GUI is a very important part of Haiku. In fact, Haiku respectively BeOS without a GUI would be unimaginable.

5.2.1. The most important aspects and elements of the Haiku GUI

In the chapter 5.1 some aspects of user-friendliness were described. Furthermore, the cognitive load theory was explained. In this chapter the user-friendliness of the Haiku graphic user interface will be analysed by using the theoretical knowledge of the previous chapter.

The GUI is a very important part of Haiku. In opposite to Linux, where the GUI is only some kind of optional add-on, the GUI is an essential part of Haiku. There is no separate windows manager in Haiku because the GUI is an integral part of this operating system.[46] Without the GUI Haiku can not be used and even the installation process of Haiku is using a graphic user interface. Although Haiku supports a POSIX compatible terminal, the operating system is meant to be mostly used by desktop users with a strong focus on the graphic user interface.

The user-friendliness of Haiku begins when starting the installation of the operating system.
The installation of Haiku is easy and user-friendly. It is completely supported by a graphic user interface and graphical dialogues. The system tries to detect most of the hardware and makes most of the system configurations without disturbing and asking the user. The user just has to do a few configurations, such as the time zone, the language setting of the keyboard and the preparing and selecting the hard disk partition where Haiku shall be installed. Sadly, in Haiku R1 Alpha 2 there are some technical installation problems, but they will be hopefully removed in later versions of Haiku. Nevertheless, when considering that it is only an early Alpha version, the installation is very user friendly from my point of view.

After the installation the operating system boots and shows a clean desktop to the user. Only a few symbolic links, the folder trash, the mounted volume of the Haiku system partition and the Deskbar are visible (see graphic 4). There are no unnecessary graphical special effects. The desktop contains only the Deskbar, the trash basket, the hard disk icon and some links to documents that contain information and tutorials how to work with Haiku. As mentioned in the previous chapter, the cognitive load theory recommends a clean and simple presentation of learn content: *"Keep it simple"* and *"Less is more"*.

---

46 *Haiku, Inc.: Haiku's GUI, in the Internet: http://www.haiku-os.org/docs/userguide/en/gui.html,*
  Date: 14th August 2010

Such a clean desktop is not going to confuse a new user who has no or not many experiences with Haiku or BeOS. From the point of view of users a new operating system is something mysterious, perhaps even something scary. After booting a new operating system, a not experienced user may only want to test it and therefore he or she should not be confused or distributed with unnecessary icons, functions, information and too many visual special effects (see the principle **Suitability for the task** according to ISO 9241-10 and the recommendations of the **cognitive load theory** in the chapter 5.1). From this point of view, Haiku provides a user-friendly start and welcomes new users with a clean and simple desktop.

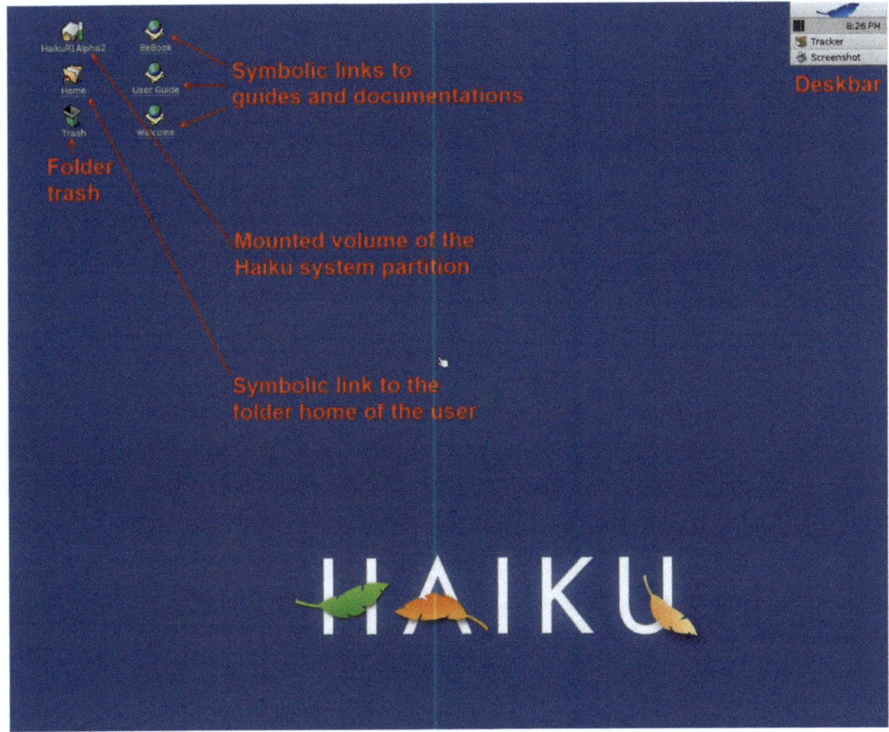

Graphic 4: Default desktop of Haiku R1 Alpha 2

As you can see in the graphic 4, there are three links to documentations.

The document **Welcome** contains some general information about the currently installed version of Haiku and some additional instructions where to get further information and how to install additional software.

The document **User Guide** describes the operating system from the point of view of the user. It is almost a complete manual with information and instructions how to use the system. The target audience is the user and not the developer. The documentation contains an overview, detailed instructions and screenshots in specific chapters about the workspaces, the graphic user interface, the file system layout, the most important applications, the shortcuts and many other things.

Finally, there is a link to the **BeBook**. This is a documentation that is interesting for the developers and programmers. It contains detailed information and some small example programs regarding the application programming interface of BeOS which consists of several kits that were mentioned in the chapter 2.2. As already mentioned in previous chapters, the goal of Haiku R1 is to reimplement most of the features of BeOS R5. Therefore the application programming interface of BeOS R5 is also more or less reimplemented in Haiku and the BeBook is not only interesting for application developers in BeOS, but also for Haiku. However, there are some changes and new things in Haiku that were different or did not exist in BeOS, such as the **Locale Kit** which is available in Haiku, but it does not exist in BeOS. Further information about this kit and other components of the Haiku application programming interface are available in the Haiku Book which is available in the internet: http://api.haiku-os.org

The links to the documentations on the desktop are an important aspects of the user-friendliness of Haiku and are an important help for users and developers to learn how to use the system respectively get an overview over the structure of the application programming interface (see the principle **Suitability for the learning** according to ISO 9241-10 in the chapter 5.1).

From the point of view of the user, the **Deskbar** (look at the upper right corner of the screen) is one of the most important parts of the operating system. It is more or less comparable with the button Start together with the Taskbar in Microsoft Windows. It consists of a menu from where other applications can be started or recently opened documents, folders or applications can be seen. Furthermore, it contains links to the system preferences where you can configure the operating system (see graphic 5). Additionally, the Deskbar contains a clock, links to some other applications, a list of currently running applications and the Deskbar offers the user many other functions, such as shutting down or restarting the system, mounting drives, showing respectively hiding **replicants** (these will be explained later in this chapter) or showing the version of the installed Haiku operating system.

Graphic 5: Preferences in the Deskbar

In the previous chapter the cognitive load theory was described. According to this theory one of the goals is to decrease or minimize the extraneous load. Haiku does this by having a clean desktop, simple visual structures and not using unnecessary visual special effects.

Furthermore, Haiku also provides fast access to the relevant data and information.

In the real world many ergonomic work environments contain three or more memory levels.

Imagine a well organized office. There is a desk (first level memory), several push loading drawers under the desk (second level memory) and some file cabinets somewhere in the room (third level memory).

The clerk will have the papers, which he uses very often, somewhere on the desk. Other papers, that he needs sometimes, will be stored in the push loading drawers under the desk. Those papers, that he does not need often, will be stored in the file cabinets.

What are the differences between the desk, the push loading drawers under the desk and the file cabinets at the walls of the room?

Firstly, there are differences regarding the capacities. The capacity of the desk is small. The capacity of the push loading drawers is much greater than the capacity of the desk, but the greatest capacity is available in the file cabinets.

Secondly, there are differences regarding the access speed. The office worker sees all documents on the desktop and needs only one hand to take them. The documents in the push loading drawers under the desk require a medium access time. The office worker has to open one or even several push loading drawers before he can look and pick up the file that he needs. The worst access speed is associated with the file cabinets that are placed somewhere in the rooms, often near the walls. The office worker has to stand up, walk to the file cabinet, open it and search for the relevant documents.

In Haiku it is more or less similar. There are several memory levels.

The desktop and the **LaunchBoxes** are the first level memory. In Haiku there are workspaces. Each workspace contains exactly one desktop. The workspaces increase the total capacity of the first level memory by providing more than one desktop to the user. The LaunchBoxes are simple applications with simple graphical forms where you can store links to other applications, documents or files in general. Normally, the user stores links to applications, documents or other files that he often uses. The user needs only one click to access the entries in a LaunchBox. Furthermore, the user can create several LaunchBoxes and all of them are configurable; the user can decide whether a specific LaunchBox is available in all workspaces or only in one specific workspace (see the principle **Suitability for individualization** according to ISO 9241-10 in the chapter 5.1).

In the example the LaunchBox Pad 1 is available in all four workspaces, but the LaunchBox Pad 2 is visible only in the first workspace (see graphic 6).

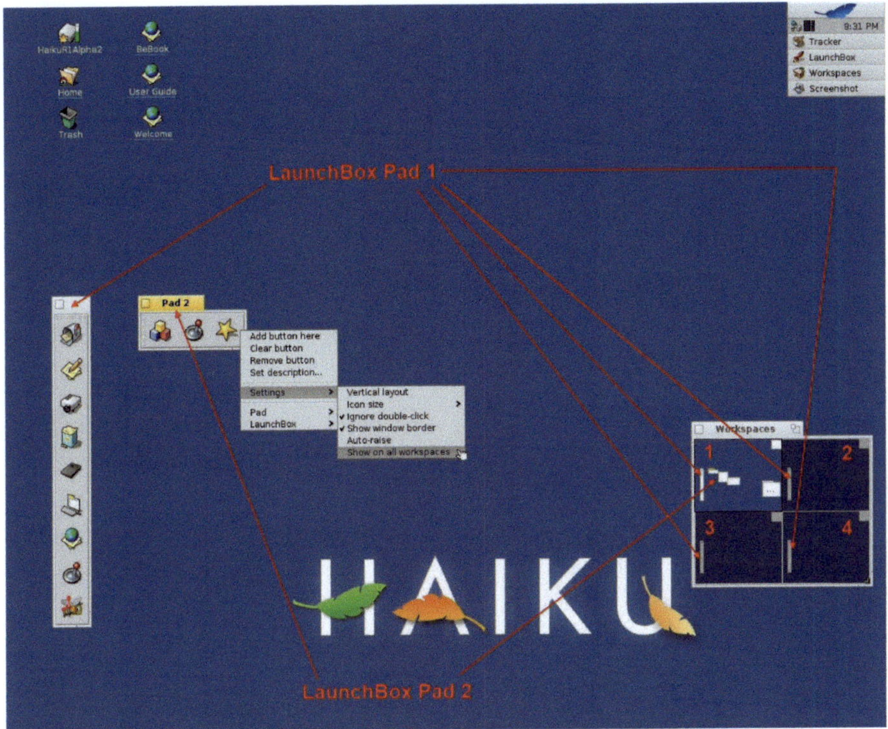

Graphic 6: LaunchBoxes in workspaces

The applications and documents in the menus of the Deskbar are located in the second level memory. The user needs only a few clicks to access them.

The documents, files and applications, that are neither accessible by using the desktop nor by using the deskbar, are accessible only by searching them on the disk. Of course, this is additional work for the user and takes much time. However, even here Haiku accelerates the search and has a focus on the user-friendliness. As already mentioned in the chapter 3, the OpenBFS supports multithreaded access to the disk which optimizes the search when two or more tasks access to the disk at the same time. Furthermore, OpenBFS supports extended file attributes, such as meta file data. This makes advanced search options possible. Of course, Haiku is a user-friendly operating system with focus on the graphic user interface. Therefore simple and common search queries can be created by using a graphical form (see graphic 7). Furthermore, the user can choose whether the query shall be automatically self-destructed after seven days or it shall be saved for a long term by selecting whether the search query is temporary or not.

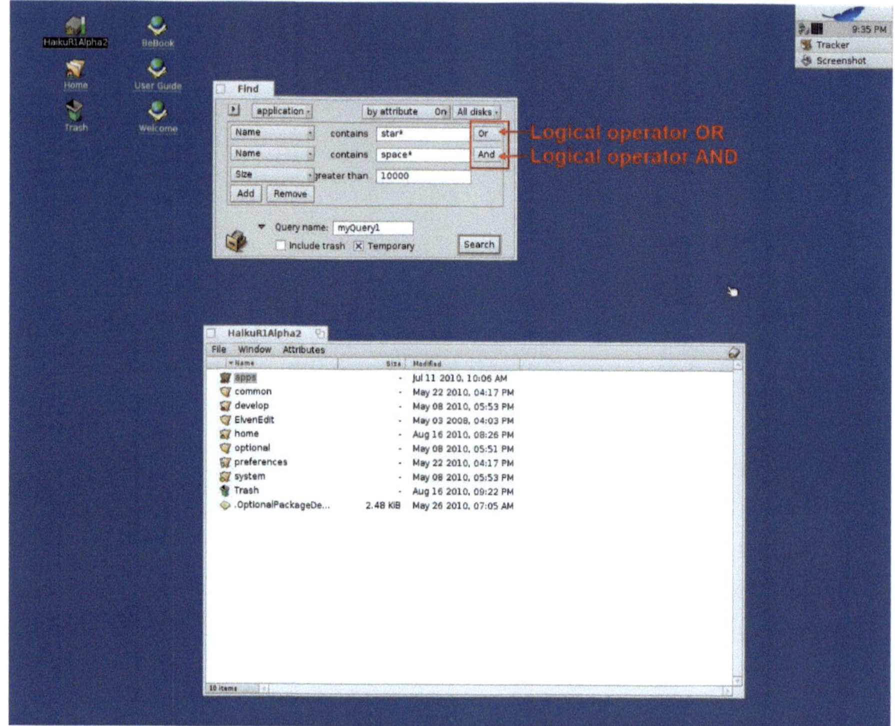

Graphic 7: Creating a search query by using the graphic query builder

The search query, which was created by using the graphic form, is automatically translated in a specific syntax (see graphic 8). Although the user can create most of the common search queries by using the graphic form, he will have to learn and use the specific search syntax if he wants to create complex queries. At the moment only the logical operators AND and OR are supported by the graphic search query builder. From my point of view, this is not enough. It would be good if additionally the logical operators NOT and XOR and the combining of them (by using brackets) were supported in future.

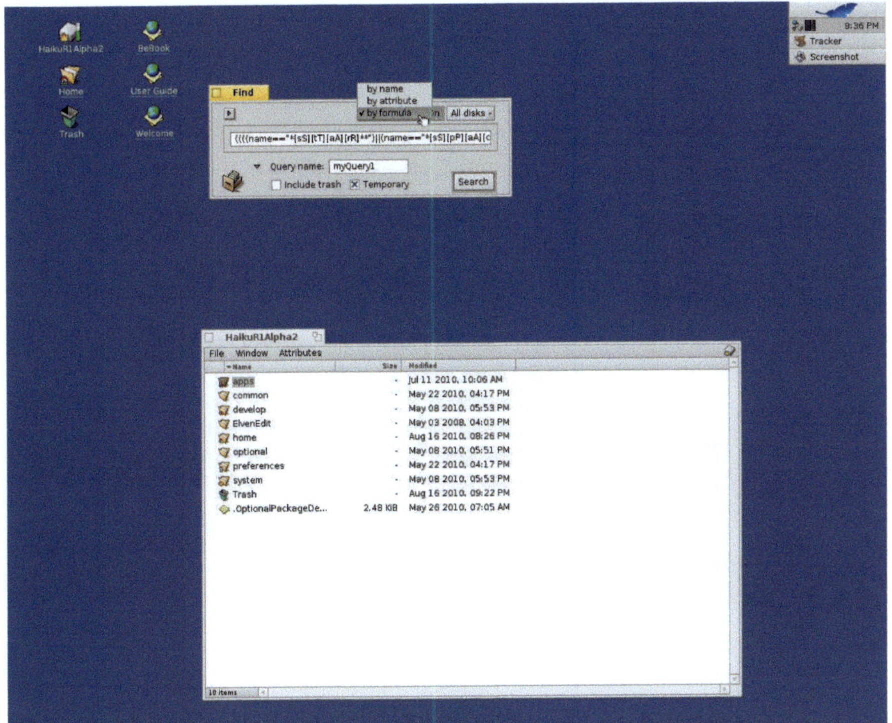

Graphic 8: Creating a search query by using the formula editor .

Nevertheless, at the moment I am using only the version Haiku R1 Alpha 2. Therefore it should not be expected too much at this early milestones. Later versions could be much more powerful and support the creation of advanced search queries by using the graphic query builder. In general, I am aware that R1 Alpha 2, an early (testing) version of Haiku, supports more search options than many other, even commercial, operating systems do.

Something quite special, which I did not see in any other operating systems before, are the replicants. Replicants are a part of an application that can be used as stand alone applications and placed on the desktop. Sometimes they are very useful. Imagine an application that tracks the activities of the CPU cores and the usage of the memory. Sometimes you are only interested in the load of the CPU cores and you are not interested in the memory usage. In this care, it would not be efficient to show both information on the screen. You would waste the limited capacity of the first level memory for information that is not useful for you. In such cases the usage of replicants could increase the density of relevant information on the desktop.

You would place only the replicant (the part of the application) that tracks the load of the CPU cores on the desktop (see the graphics 9 and 10). Please note that the teapots are distorted because the application, that creates the screenshot, is too slow to catch a screen that is refreshed with more or less 500 frames per second. Although my system uses only a VESA driver without the NVidia graphic accelerator, the rendering of the rotating GL teaplot is very fast.

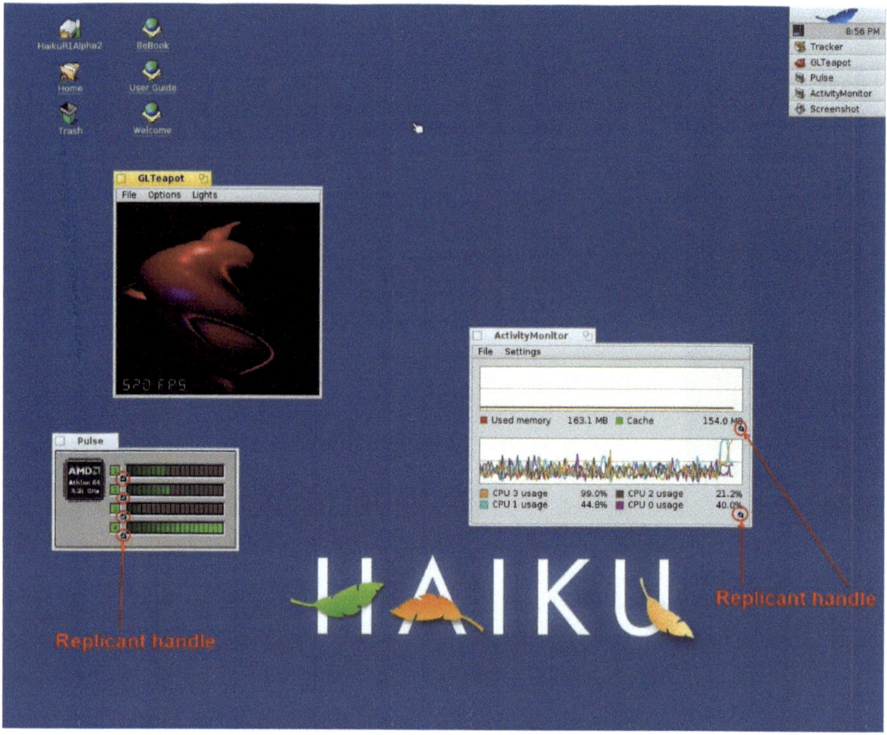

Graphic 9: Two applications that contain replicants

The application Pulse shows the load of the available CPU cores. Furthermore, the user can disable or enable a CPU core by clinking on the number of the CPU core. In the example, there are four CPU cores because an AMD Phenom II X4 processor is used.

The application Activity Monitor shows the load of the processor cores and the usage of the memory by displaying both on diagrams.

Both applications, the application Pulse and the application Activity Monitor, support the usage of replicants. The replicants can be placed on the desktop by using the direct manipulation method *drag and drop* on the replicant handles.

Graphic 10: Replicants placed on the desktop

The replicants are not only showing some data, but they are also interactive. For example, you can enable or disable a CPU core by clicking on the number of the CPU core. In the example which is displayed in the graphic 10, the CPU cores 1 and 4 are disabled and the CPU cores 2 and 3 are enabled.

The replicants are a realization of the principle **Suitability for the task** according to ISO 9241-10 because the user has the opportunity to see only relevant information. From the point of view of the user, the replicants increase the **density of relevant information** on the desktop by making it possible to show and use only the relevant parts of an application. Therefore the first level memory becomes more efficient.

Here you see the power of Haiku regarding the first level memory: while the work spaces increase the capacity of the first level memory, the replicants increase the efficiency of the first level memory.

The two principles **Transparency and Self-Descriptiveness** and **conformity with user expectations** (see ISO 9241-10 in the previous chapter) are also fulfilled by Haiku.

Most symbols, icons and navigation principles are more or less similar to the elements of dialogues in popular operating systems such as Microsoft Windows. Therefore they are in conformity with the user expectations; most users have experience with the operating system Microsoft Windows and expect that the dialogues work more or less in a similar way like in Microsoft Windows.

However, there are some differences, especially regarding the shortcuts. Even such often used shortcuts for Copy and Paste are different in Haiku. Instead of Control C respectively Control V the equivalent shortcuts in Haiku are Alt C respectively Alt V. This may be confusing for a new user, but it is just a question of time until he or she will become familiar with the shortcuts. They are described in the User Manual which can be accessed by double clicking the corresponding link on the desktop. After a while the dialogues become conform with the user expectations because they are very consistent and the same icons, symbols and other elements of a graphic form have the same or similar meanings in other graphic forms, too. Furthermore, is it really necessary that all operating systems have the same shortcuts for often used operations, such as Copy and Paste?

On the one hand, it makes it easier for new users.

But on the other hand, there is no special reason why Control C respectively Control V are used by many operating systems. For example, people with short fingers may prefer Alt C respectively Alt V because the distance between the key Alt and the keys C and V is shorter than between these two keys and the key Control.

The most important aspect regarding the principle conformity with user expectations is the consistence of the usage of navigation, icons, symbols and other graphical elements in different dialogues. This requirement is fulfilled by Haiku.

As already explained in the previous chapter, the speed of the response is very important from the point of view of users. In this field Haiku is very powerful. The response speeds of the Haiku GUI are amazing. Even when using only a slow system, for example a 1 GHz CPU, 1 GB RAM and a cheap graphic card in VESA mode, all menus in the Deskbar open in less than one second (unprepared response) or even in less than 0.1 seconds (psychological moment).

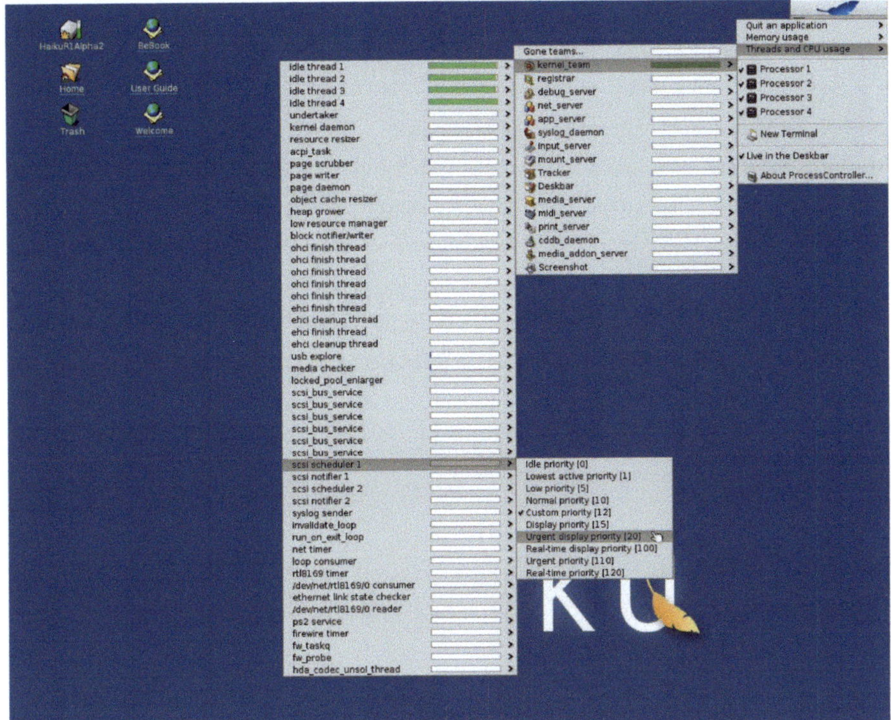

Graphic 11: Priorities of running processes

Furthermore, the user can change the priority of running processes (see graphic 11).

By doing this, the response speed of specific processes can be optimized and adapted to the individual preferences of the user. These changes can be easily done by using the **ProcessController** that can be accessed by clicking on the diagram icon in the Deskbar. Sadly, any changes of the priorities of running processes are lost after the process is closed or the system restarts. Therefore the changes are only temporary. It would be a useful feature, if a user could save these changes and create priority profiles which could be used depending on the current work or usage behaviour of the user. Sadly, such a feature is not supported by the current version of the ProcessController.

Furthermore, there is no warning before changing the priorities of processes. A not experienced user could cause serious problems by selecting too high or too low priorities for specific processes. This could be dangerous, especially because an undo function is also missing, and this is opposite to the principle of **error tolerance** according to ISO 9241-10.

In summary, Haiku is a very user-friendly desktop operating system that is almost completely based on graphical dialogues and windows.

It is easy to use, fulfils almost all aspects of ISO 9241-10 and Haiku is very fast in both: boot speeds and response times of the graphical user interface.

Of course, there are some issues regarding the user friendliness, such as the dangers that could occur because of the unlimited user permissions regarding the configuration options of the priorities of the running tasks. However, such problems are more or less normal for an alpha version of an operating system.

Further improvements in fields of user-friendliness are planned for future versions of Haiku. Ideas are discussed in the project Glass Elevator which is the right place for discussing and documenting ideas for the release 2 and later.

5.2.2. Technical implementation of the GUI with the Interface Kit

The Interface Kit plays the main role in fields of development of graphic user interfaces in BeOS and Haiku. It provides a structure for these three operations which are essential for the development of interactive GUI based applications in Haiku respectively BeOS:

- Managing a set of windows

- Drawing within the windows

- Response to the actions of users[47]

The two most important classes are **BWindow** and **BView**. A BWindow object represents a window of an application. Every window is represented by a unique BWindow object. A BWindow object communicates directly with the Application Server. However, a BApplication object must be created before the first BWindow object is created because the constructor of the BApplication object establishes the initial connection to the Application Server.

Every window contains at least one view. A view is a rectangular area within a window. Every view is represented by a unique BView object. Such an object supports drawing and managing interface messages within the rectangle area. The BWindow object can display rendered images, but it is not able to draw them. Therefore each BWindow needs views that are responsible for the drawing. Inside the content box of a view several objects can be placed, such as BBox, BScrollBar, BListView, BButton, BMenu and many others (see graphic 12).

Nevertheless, there is one exception. When constructing a BWindow object, then it automatically creates a special view which is called the **top view**. The size of the top view is exactly the same as the size of the content of the window. This special view does not draw or respond to messages. The top view is used to connect the window to the views which are children of the top view. The top view is on the top of the hierarchy. Every view, except the top view, has exactly one parent, but it can have several children (see graphics 13 and 14).

When a new BView object is created, it does not belong to any window. The view becomes a part of a window by making it a child of an other view that already belongs to the specific window. The method *AddChild()* of the **BView** object is responsible for this. There is also a method with the same name inside the BWindow object. This method is used to set a view as a child of the top view of the window.

---

47 *The Be Development Team (1997): Be Developer's Guide, O'Reilly & Associates, page 331*

Interface Kit Inheritance Hierarchy

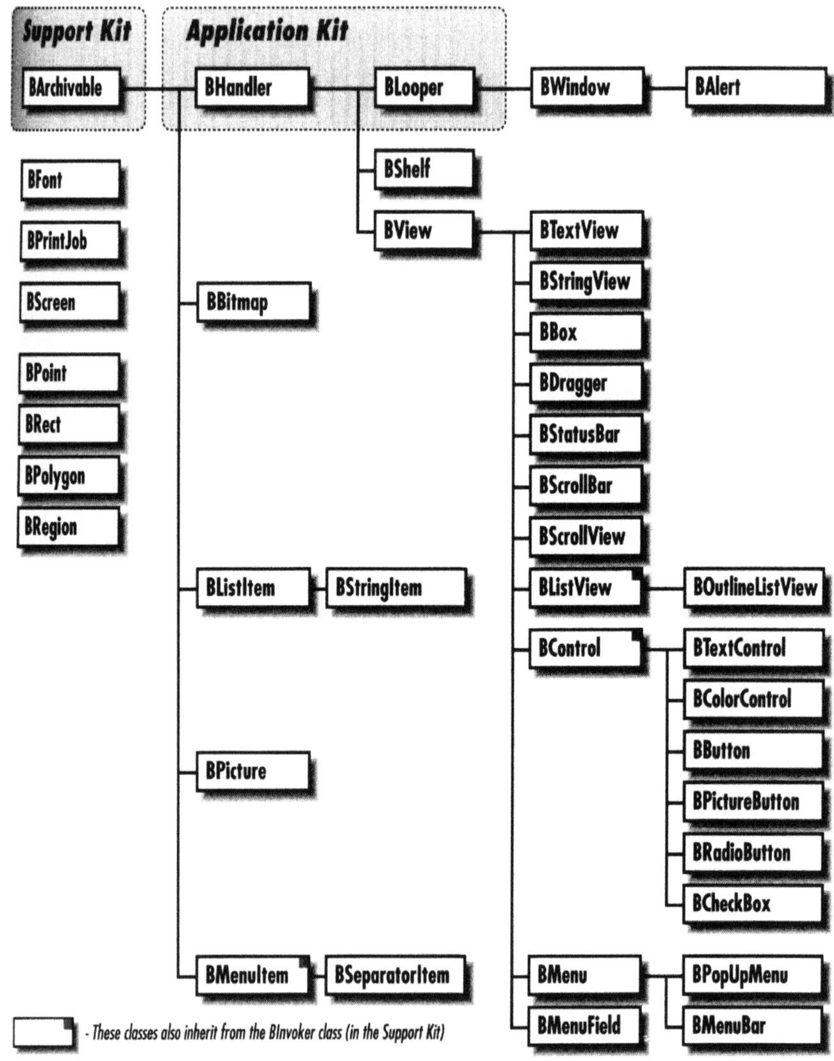

Graphic 12: Hierarchy of classes of the Interface Kit[48]

---

48 *The Be Development Team (1997): Be Developer's Guide, O'Reilly & Associates, page 329*

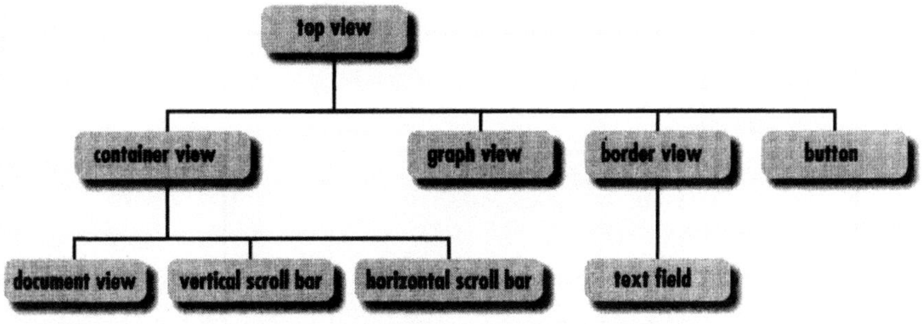

(Graphic 13: The hierarchy of views)[49]

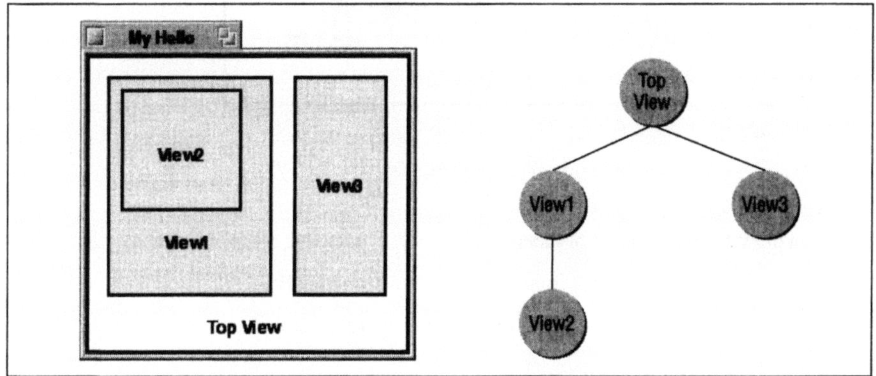

Graphic 14: Views in a window[50]

A child view can be placed anywhere inside the parent view. The child view has a coordinate system of itself (see the graphic 15). In this example the child view (grey rectangle) has a width of 180 units and a height of 135 units. When viewed from the outside, this means from the point of view of the parent view, the top left corner of the child view's frame rectangle has the coordinates 90 and 60. But when viewed from the inside of the child view, it has a bounds rectangle with the coordinates left 0, top 0, right 180 and bottom 135. When the child view is moved within the parent view, then the coordinates of the frame rectangle change, but the coordinates of the bound rectangle do not change. When the contents inside the child view are scrolled, then the coordinates of the bound rectangle change, but the frame rectangle is not changed. The bound rectangle and the inner coordinate system of the child view are in most cases used when placing content, such as buttons, boxes and many others, inside the child view.

---

49 *The Be Development Team (1997): Be Developer's Guide, O'Reilly & Associates, page 333*
50 *Sydow, D. P.: Programming the Be Operating System, O'Reilly & Associates, page 118*

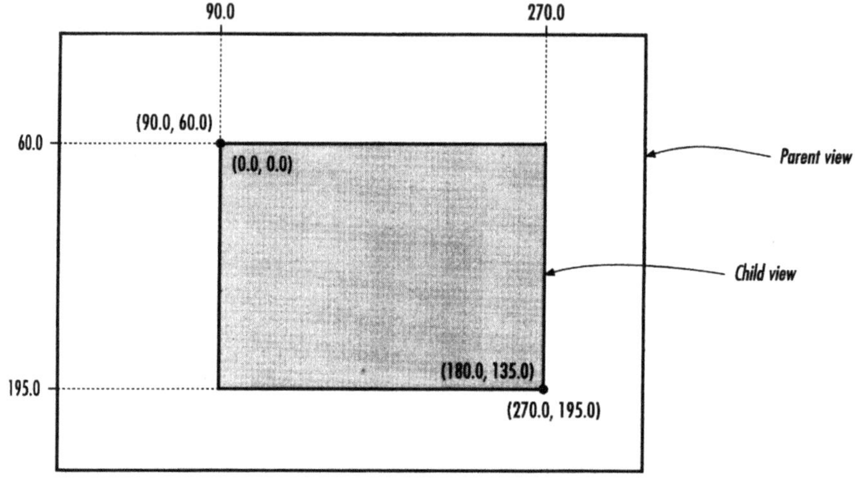

Graphic 15: Coordinate systems of views[51]

Views can draw by using this set of functions:

- *CopyBits()* copies an image from a location A to a location B.

- *DrawBitmap()* creates an image by using a bitmap as the data source.

- *DrawChar()* draws one character.

- *DrawPicture()* executes a set of instructions for drawing that are recorded.

- *DrawString()* draws a string that contains several characters.

- The Fill methods, such as *FillArc()*, *FillEllipse()*, *FillPolygon()*, *FillRect()* and some others, fill shapes that are closed.

- The Stroke methods, such as *StrokeArc()*, *StrokeEllipse()*, *StrokeLine()* and some others, stroke shapes.

- Sets of lines with the same width, but optionally with different colours, can be drawn by using the methods *BeginLineArray()*, *AddLine()* and *EndLineArray()*.

There are several graphic parameters that can be set to a specific view, such as font, pen size, clipping region, drawing mode and some others. Further information is available in advanced BeOS and Haiku documentations.

---

51 *The Be Development Team (1997): Be Developer's Guide, O'Reilly & Associates, page 335*

The BWindow respectively BView objects are not only responsible for rendering respectively drawing images, but they are also responsible for the handling of the interface messages and responding to the actions of users that are generated by the usage of the keyboard and the mouse. Some of the messages are directed at specific views, some are belonging to the complete window. Further information is available in advanced BeOS and Haiku documentations.[52]

5.3. The capabilities for multimedia applications and games

In the 1990s BeOS was famous because of the great multimedia capabilities and high performance playback of videos. In the chapter 4 many features of BeOS are described.

However, many years passed and Windows became more and more powerful in fields of multimedia. Haiku Release 1 is still trying to reimplement the features of BeOS Release 5, an operating system that was released in March 2000. Microsoft had about ten years time to extend the multimedia features of Windows and was very successful.

Current versions of popular multimedia software products, such as Adobe Premiere, Adobe Photoshop, 3D Studio Max, Maya and many others, are mostly only available for Windows and perhaps for Mac OS. Even Linux is not supported by all professional multimedia software products. This is a big problem for Haiku. Although Haiku has advanced multimedia capabilities and is a very fast operating system in many fields, there is a lack of professional up-to-date multimedia software products that are compatible with Haiku.

Therefore Haiku and BeOS are not very useful multimedia operating systems from the point of view of many professional designers. The situation looks even worse, when we take into account that drivers are not available for many hardware devices, such as up-to-date graphic cards, many video capturing cards and other multimedia devices. For example, the NVidia drivers for Haiku support only graphic cards up to the NVidia GeForce 7 series which are already some years old and not recommended for many new, hardware demanding 3D modelling software products and computer games. Native drivers for most of the modern graphic cards are not available for Haiku respectively BeOS. Therefore Haiku uses a generic VESA driver that supports almost all graphic cards, but without unveiling the full power of the graphic card. The actually used graphic card driver can be detected by entering the command *listimage | grep accelerant* in the Haiku shell.

The VESA driver is used for most modern graphic cards because the specific drivers for the graphic cards are not available for Haiku respectively BeOS. Although the VESA driver of Haiku is very

---

52 *The Be Development Team (1997): Be Developer's Guide, O'Reilly & Associates, p. 340 to 349*

fast, it is, of course, not able to support all the features and acceleration capabilities of the specific graphic card. This problem affects not only some multimedia software products but also many computer games. Of course, this is not a problem of the operating system itself because drivers for the hardware devices are in most cases provided by the manufacturers of the hardware devices or the built-in chipsets, but from the point of view of the user this is a serious issue.

On long term, the success of Haiku will depend, among other things, on the availability of drivers for modern hardware devices in future. One hope is that in future more hardware devices could be perhaps supported by open source drivers, but this also depends on the policies and strategies of the manufacturers of the hardware devices, whether they will publish the source code of their drivers or not. However, this does not only affect Haiku but also many other operating systems besides the market leader Microsoft Windows, for example FreeBSD and various Linux distributions.

Nevertheless, Haiku is already able to provide multimedia experiences to the user. Those users, that do not need professional multimedia software products, could be already now satisfied with the multimedia features of Haiku and already available multimedia software packages. Most widely used video and audio codecs such as AVI, AIFF, ASF, MP3, MPEG, QuickTime and WAV are supported by the Media Kit or additional software packages. The popular Video LAN VLC player is also available for Haiku, although it is not the latest version of the player. However, it is no problem to simultaneously play several videos without any performance issues and system instabilities.

Simple, yet quite powerful, graphic editing software is also available. One of the most popular is WonderBrush that is surely no competition for Photoshop, but it may be suitable for users that just want to edit their vocation photographies and prepare some images for their personal profile on various social networks, such as Facebook. Such people do not need all the advanced features of professional and expensive graphic editing tools like Adobe Photoshop.

When taking this all into account, then it seems that Haiku is not interesting for professional multimedia designers, but it could become a powerful and very user-friendly operating system for low-budget desktop computers, netbooks and notebooks.

Nowadays computer games are one of the best examples of the intensive usage of multimedia. Most modern computer games contain amazing 2D and 3D graphics, high quality music and sound effects and (almost) Hollywood-like in-game videos. The Media Kit and Midi Kit provide powerful multimedia capabilities, but games also contain many real time calculated animations that have to be created very fast in order to look smooth (at least 25 frames per second are necessary).

In case of 2D graphics, very fast drawing methods are necessary. In BeOS and Haiku this fast drawing of graphics and many other features are provided by the Game Kit, a part of the API. The Game Kit will be described in the next pages.

In case of 3D games, advanced graphical features are required. One of the standard libraries for 3D is OpenGL. As already mentioned in the chapter 2.2, OpenGL is available by using the OpenGL Kit. Because OpenGL is a standard that is not specific for BeOS respectively Haiku, it will not be described in this thesis.

The Game Kit provides features that are useful for developers of computer games. It contains two main types of features:

High-performance audio:

There are several classes that enable the developer to use high-performance audio playback in applications and computer games.

Low-level graphic access:

Traditionally, when an operating system is displaying images on the monitor, it has to capture and preprocess every frame of information, send it to the graphic card and then wait until it gets the final image from the graphic card in order it can be displayed inside a specific window.

This process takes much time because it requires much processing power of the CPU. Regarding games, this method is not a good solution because animations have to be smooth (at least 25 frames per second) and the processing power of the CPU is also needed for other tasks, such as artificial intelligence, calculations of in-game physics, collision detection and many others. Therefore the Game Kit contains the two classes *BWindowScreen* and *BDirectWindow* which enable the developer to directly access the frame buffer of the graphic card in order to largely bypass the operating system in this process and decrease the CPU load. This process is called DMA (Direct Memory Access). The main difference between these two classes is that BWindowScreen is used to draw on the entire screen by bypassing the window system of the Application Server, while BDirectWindow can be used to draw in a window.

If using a BWindowScreen object, then it has a direct access to the driver of the graphic card. It can use the driver-implemented drawing functions and directly manipulate the frame buffer.

If using a BDirectWindow, then two modes are available: the *window mode* and the *full-screen (exclusive)* mode. In both cases the direct access to the frame buffer of the graphic card is enabled, but there are differences regarding the behaviour of the used window. In full-screen mode the window is full-screen, always in the focus and in the foreground. No other window can pop up in front of the full-screen window. In window mode, the BDirectWindow looks more or less like a normal BWindow. Other windows may pop up and be moved in front of it. The mode can be changed by using the method *SetFullScreen()*. To enable full-screen (exclusive) mode the value *true* has to be passed to the method. The window mode is set by passing the value *false*. The currently used mode can be detected by calling the function *IsFullScreen()* that will return the value *true* in case of full-screen (exclusively) mode respectively *false* in case of window mode.[53]

The demo Chart, that is included in (almost) all BeOS and Haiku distributions, can be used to measure the performance benefits of BDirectWindow compared to the traditional BitmapDraw method that does not use the advantages of Direct Memory Access (DMA). Here are some benchmark results that I achieved with my personal desktop computer.

System configuration:

Haiku R1 Alpha 2 GCC2 Hybrid Revision 36769, Kernel 8th May 2010,

PC with AMD Phenom II X4 3.2 GHz, Gigabyte GA-MA790XT-UD4P mainboard,

4 GB DDR3 1333 RAM, 250 GB 3.5" 7200 rps hard disk WDC WD5000AAKS SATA,

NVidia GeForce 9500 GT graphic card with 512 MB video memory using a VESA driver

Desktop screen resolution: 1280 x 1024 pixel, colours 32 bits per pixel.

General Chart application configuration:

Display stars in all colours. Star density is 10. Type of space is chaos.

Type of animation is free motion. Special effect novas is activated. Use full screen.

Results of the benchmarks:

Configuration	CPU load in percentage
DrawBitmap, 1 thread	23.8
DrawBitmap, 2 threads	23.5
DirectWindow, 1 thread	0.8
DirectWindow, 2 threads	0.6

The results show that there are amazing performance benefits when using DirectWindow instead of DrawBitmap in the benchmark.

---

53 *The Be Development Team (1998): Advanced Topics, O'Reilly & Associates, p. 183 to 210*

6. Empirical research about the Haiku community

In opposite to the previous chapters, where the sources of data were books and documentations, in this chapter empirical data will be analysed. The source of data is my online survey that was announced on the official Haiku website and several other Haiku or BeOS related websites.

6.1. General information about the survey

The online survey consists of 24 questions. All questions were optional, this means, that the respondents could freely choose whether they want to answer a question or not.
Furthermore, the respondents could be anonymous. Neither the name nor the address were asked in the survey. The e-mail address was an optional entry.

The online survey was announced in the news section or in other sections of several websites, including the official Haiku website http://www.haiku-os.org and a popular news website about Haiku: http://www.haiku-gazette.de
Furthermore, it was announced in the Haiku General Mailing List. The survey was online from 7th May 2010 to 16th October 2010.

The online survey was technically implemented by using ASP, XHTML, CSS and a Microsoft Access database. ASP was my personal preference because I already had many experiences in programming dynamic websites with ASP. The Microsoft Access database is a simple, yet powerful solution for the small amount of data that will be gathered by the online survey. Furthermore, Access can be used as a data source for the statistical software SPSS which is used for the data analyses. From the beginning on I expected that many respondents will use various operating systems and that their interest in Haiku respectively BeOS is a consequence of their fascination for operating systems in general. Therefore it was very important to take care about the cross browser compatibility of the online survey. This was done by avoiding the usage of JavaScript, Flash and any other technologies that require Plug-Ins or very special web browsers. Furthermore, the XHTML Strict code and the CSS code of the online survey website are valid according to the W3C validation services.

One important goal was to be able to detect multiple participation by the same respondent. In most cases such phenomena are not a wilful sabotage but simply a technical problem because of a slow connection to the internet, delayed reaction of the server or other reasons. In such cases people sometimes press twice or multiple times the submit button at the end of the survey. The consequence is that the answers are saved twice or multiple times in the data base. Therefore each respondent gets a session id that is automatically created by the ASP program while the online survey website is created and sent to the client. The session id is unique for each client and consists of a random number and the number of remaining seconds until the begin of the next century.

Dim MySessionID

Randomize

*MySessionID = Int((Rnd * 10000)) + 1 & DateDiff("s", Now(), cdate("1/1/2100 00:00:00"))*

This unique session id is sent, after pressing the submit button, by using the method post from the client back to the server and saved together with the answers of the respondent in the Access database. By searching for data entries that do not have a unique session id in the Access database, the multiple results can be found and manually deleted. This was the first step of the data clean up.

Additionally, the ASP code saves the duration (in seconds) from the loading of the website until pressing the submit button in the Access data base. In the second step of the data clean up some data entries with durations of less than 60 seconds were manually removed because such entries are often created by robots or by curious people just for fun. Nevertheless, not all entries with durations of less than 60 seconds were removed because in some cases the data seems to be valid and generated by a real person and not by a internet bot. Therefore I had manually to look and decide which result is valid and which one is invalid.

The median value of the duration is equal to 689 seconds. When I created the survey, I expected that the people will need about 10 minutes to answer it. The median duration was about 11 minutes that is not far away from my original expectations.

By processing the two above described clean up steps, the sample size decreased from 1332 to 1296. This cleaned up data is used for data analyses.

6.2. Results of the survey

In this chapter the results of the survey are analysed and interpreted. While in the first subchapter all the questions of the survey and the corresponding aggregated results are presented, further and advanced statistical methods are used to search for correlations in the following subchapter.

6.2.1. Questions and answers

Question 1: How much are you interested in Haiku OS in general?

O not at all (1)   O a little bit (2)   O medium (3)   O fairly (4)   O very much (5)

Results:

Statistics

InterestedInHaikuR

N	Valid	1291
	Missing	5
Mean		4.2866
Std. Error of Mean		.02477
Median		5.0000
Mode		5.00
Std. Deviation		.89006
Sum		5534.00

InterestedInHaikuR

		Frequency	Percent	Valid Percent	Cumulative Percent
Valid	1.00	4	.3	.3	.3
	2.00	73	5.6	5.7	6.0
	3.00	136	10.5	10.5	16.5
	4.00	414	31.9	32.1	48.6
	5.00	664	51.2	51.4	100.0
	Total	1291	99.6	100.0	
Missing	System	5	.4		
Total		1296	100.0		

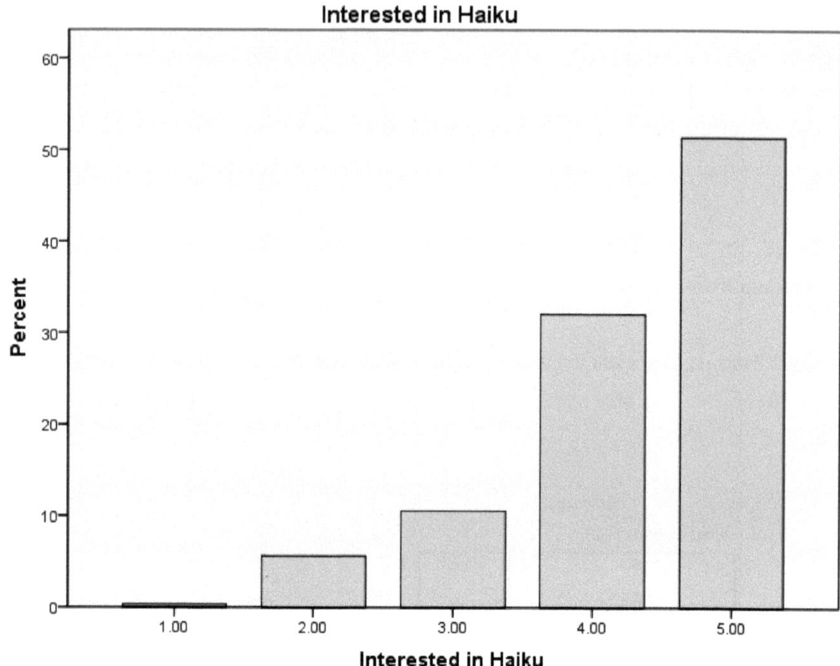

Graphic 16: Survey results regarding the interest in Haiku

There is a great interest in Haiku. The mean is about 4.3 ("fairly interested in Haiku") and the median is equivalent to 5 ("very much interested in Haiku").

Question 2: How much are you interested in BeOS in general?

O not at all (1)   O a little bit (2)   O medium (3)   O fairly (4)   O very much (5)

Results:

Statistics

InterestedInBeOSR

N	Valid	1287
	Missing	9
Mean		3.4662
Std. Error of Mean		.03581
Median		4.0000
Mode		5.00
Std. Deviation		1.28464
Sum		4461.00

InterestedInBeOSR

		Frequency	Percent	Valid Percent	Cumulative Percent
Valid	1.00	96	7.4	7.5	7.5
	2.00	253	19.5	19.7	27.1
	3.00	253	19.5	19.7	46.8
	4.00	325	25.1	25.3	72.0
	5.00	360	27.8	28.0	100.0
	Total	1287	99.3	100.0	
Missing	System	9	.7		
Total		1296	100.0		

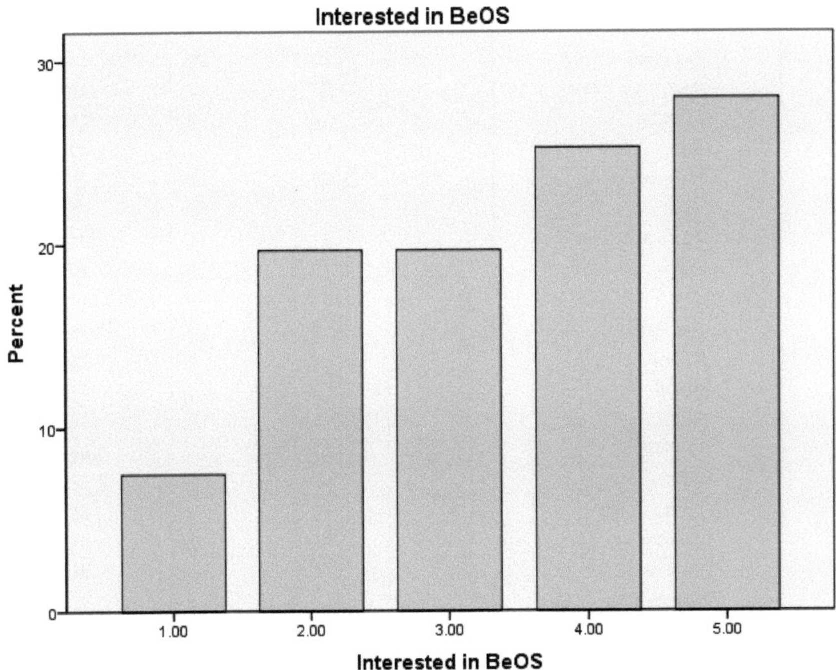

Graphic 17: Survey results regarding the interest in BeOS

There is a fairly interest in BeOS. The mean is about 3.47 ("medium interested in Haiku") and the median is equivalent to 4 ("fairly interested in Haiku"). The people are more interested in Haiku than in BeOS. This result is no wonder because BeOS does not support many new hardware devices and many users hope that Haiku will become a good and proud successor of BeOS.

Page 73

Question 3: What is your most favourit operating system for x86 compatible computers?

Please select the operating system that you like most of all.

It is not important whether you use it or not.

Results:

Favourit OS

		Frequency	Percent	Valid Percent	Cumulative Percent
Valid	Arch	64	4.9	4.9	4.9
	BeOSHaiku	437	33.7	33.7	38.7
	BSD (FreeBSD, PC-BSD or some other BSD)	68	5.2	5.2	43.9
	DEBIAN	54	4.2	4.2	48.1
	Fedora	23	1.8	1.8	49.8
	KUBUNTU	18	1.4	1.4	51.2
	Linux (some other)	51	3.9	3.9	55.2
	MacOS X or newer	204	15.7	15.7	70.9
	Mandriva	11	.8	.8	71.8
	Mint	13	1.0	1.0	72.8
	No answer	13	1.0	1.0	73.8
	Other	23	1.8	1.8	75.5
	PCLinuxOS	1	.1	.1	75.6
	Puppy	3	.2	.2	75.8
	QNX	8	.6	.6	76.5
	Red Hat	2	.2	.2	76.6
	Sabayon	2	.2	.2	76.8
	SkyOS	4	.3	.3	77.1
	SUSE	23	1.8	1.8	78.9
	UBUNTU	133	10.3	10.3	89.1
	Unix	6	.5	.5	89.6
	Windows 2000	4	.3	.3	89.9
	Windows 7	61	4.7	4.7	94.6
	Windows 95/98	4	.3	.3	94.9
	Windows Some Other	1	.1	.1	95.0
	Windows Vista	2	.2	.2	95.1
	Windows XP	42	3.2	3.2	98.4
	XUBUNTU	8	.6	.6	99.0
	ZETA	13	1.0	1.0	100.0
	Total	1296	100.0	100.0	

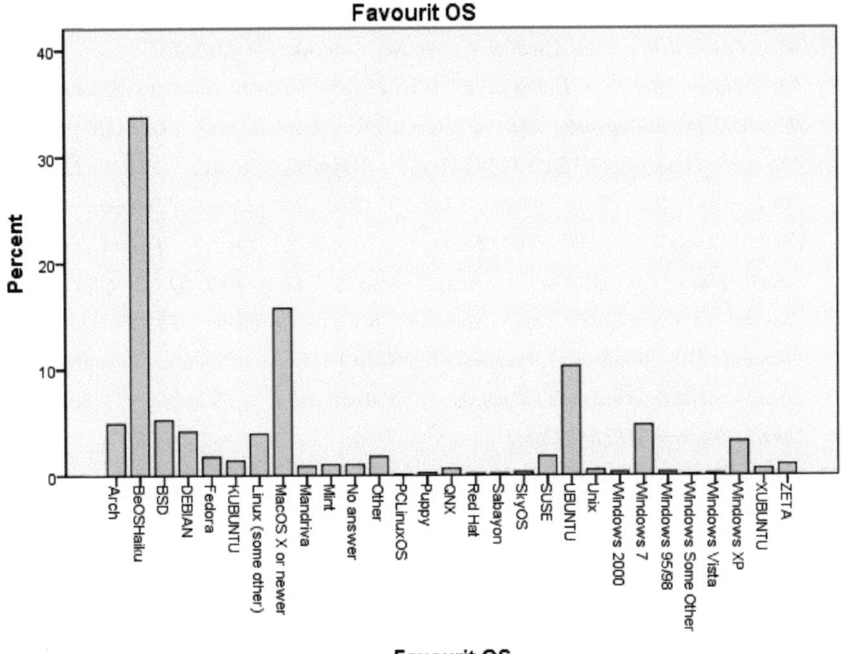

Graphic 18: Survey results regarding the favourit operating system

The most favourit operating system is BeOS or Haiku ("BeOSHaiku"). ZETA, that is also inspired by BeOS, is not popular. Only about one percent of the persons answered that ZETA is their most favourit operating system. Besides Haiku and BeOS the operating systems Linux (especially UBUNTU), MacOS X (or newer) and Windows (especially Windows 7 and windows XP) are popular among the asked persons. One reason for the quite good result regarding MacOS X could be the fact that originally BeOS was inspired by MacOS and that both operating systems have a focus on multimedia capabilities.

The above displayed statistics include the names of the operating systems and their distribution releases respectively versions. However, it is also interesting to see which operating system families are popular. Therefore the data was recoded by using this syntax in SPSS 19 for both variables: FavouritOS and MostUsedOS (see question 4):

STRING FavouritOSFamilyR MostUsedOSFamilyR (A80).

RECODE FavouritOS MostUsedOS ('?'='No answer') (MISSING='No answer') ('BeOSHaiku'='BeOS or Haiku or ZETA') ('ZETA'='BeOS or Haiku or ZETA') ('BSD (FreeBSD, PC-BSD or some other BSD)'='BSD') ('Arch'='Linux') ('DEBIAN'='Linux') ('Fedora'='Linux') ('KUBUNTU'='Linux') ('Mandriva'='Linux') ('Mint'='Linux') ('PCLinuxOS'='Linux') ('Puppy'='Linux') ('Red Hat'='Linux') ('Sabayon'='Linux') ('SUSE'='Linux') ('UBUNTU'='Linux') ('XUBUNTU'='Linux') ('Linux (some other)'='Linux') ('MacOS X or newer'='MacOS X or newer') ('QNX'='QNX RTOS') ('SkyOS'='SkyOS') ('Unix'='Unix (besides BSD)') ('Windows 95/98'='Windows') ('Windows ME'='Windows') ('Windows 2000'='Windows') ('Windows XP'='Windows') ('Windows Vista'='Windows') ('Windows 7'='Windows') ('Windows Some Other'='Windows') (ELSE=Copy)

INTO FavouritOSFamilyR MostUsedOSFamilyR.
EXECUTE.

The favourit operating system families are BeOS/Haiku/Zeta (about 35 percent), Linux (between 31 and 32 percent) and MacOS X or newer (almost 16 percent). Windows is not very popular (about 9 percent). However, when looking at the results of the next question regarding the most used operating system, the ranking looks very different.

Question 4: What operating system do you mostly use on x86 compatible computers?

Please select the operating system that you use most of the time.

It is not important whether you like it or not.

Results:

Most used OS

		Frequency	Percent	Valid Percent	Cumulative Percent
Valid	Arch	70	5.4	5.4	5.4
	BeOSHaiku	35	2.7	2.7	8.1
	BSD (FreeBSD, PC-BSD or some other BSD)	19	1.5	1.5	9.6
	DEBIAN	50	3.9	3.9	13.4
	Fedora	29	2.2	2.2	15.7
	KUBUNTU	20	1.5	1.5	17.2
	Linux (some other)	63	4.9	4.9	22.1
	MacOS X or newer	222	17.1	17.1	39.2
	Mandriva	11	.8	.8	40.0
	Mint	13	1.0	1.0	41.0
	No answer	13	1.0	1.0	42.1
	Other	1	.1	.1	42.1
	PCLinuxOS	1	.1	.1	42.2
	Puppy	1	.1	.1	42.3
	Red Hat	5	.4	.4	42.7
	Sabayon	6	.5	.5	43.1
	SUSE	16	1.2	1.2	44.4
	UBUNTU	184	14.2	14.2	58.6
	Unix	1	.1	.1	58.6
	Windows 2000	8	.6	.6	59.3
	Windows 7	223	17.2	17.2	76.5
	Windows 95/98	1	.1	.1	76.5
	Windows Some Other	3	.2	.2	76.8
	Windows Vista	39	3.0	3.0	79.8
	Windows XP	241	18.6	18.6	98.4
	XUBUNTU	18	1.4	1.4	99.8
	ZETA	3	.2	.2	100.0
	Total	1296	100.0	100.0	

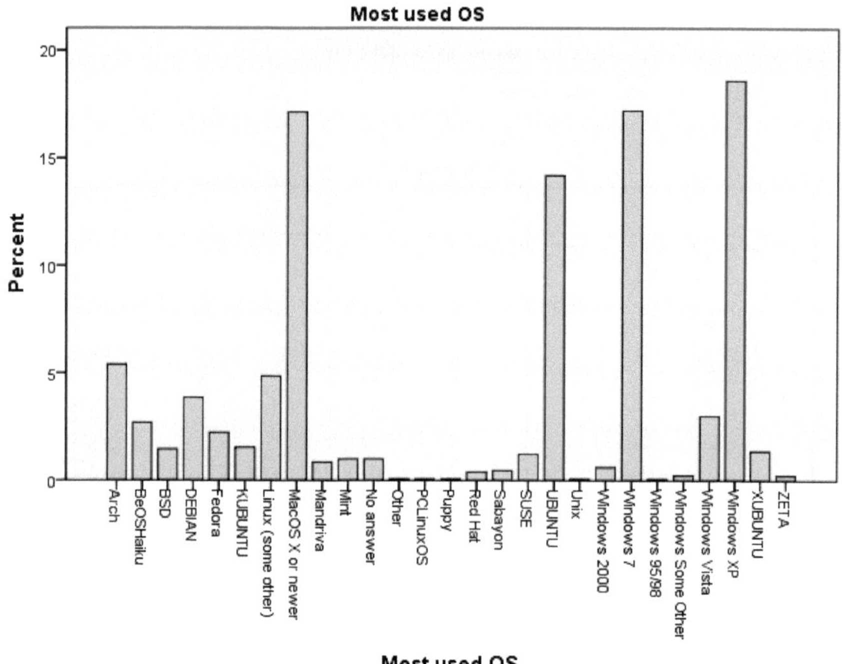

Graphic 19: Survey results regarding the most used operating system

Although about 34 percent of the people answered that Haiku or BeOS is their favourit operating system, less than three percent of the respondents use them most of all operating systems. However, this is no wonder because BeOS is old and does not support many new hardware devices and the currently newest version of Haiku is still an Alpha version that is officially not recommended to be used for productive purposes. The most used operating systems are Windows, Linux and MacOS.

When looking at the operating systems families instead at the versions and distribution releases of the operating systems (regarding the RECODE syntax, please see the previous question 3), the results show the dominating position of Microsoft Windows (about 40 percent). About 38 percent of the respondents mostly use Linux. MacOS X or newer is the most used operating system of about 17 percent of the asked people. Although 34 percent of the respondents answered that Haiku or BeOS is their favourit operating system, the operating system family of BeOS, Haiku and Zeta is the most used by only about 3 percent of the asked persons.

Question 5: Which of these operating systems do you use at least once per week on any kind of computers?

Multiple choices are possible.

<u>Results:</u>

Totally 1290 valid answers were received. Valid answers are defined by the condition that at least one of the multiple choices (including the answer "other") has to be selected. This is a useful condition to detect whether somebody answered this question or avoided to answer it. As already mentioned, all questions are optional.

Windows	1021	79.1 percent
Linux	953	73.9 percent
MacOS	465	36.0 percent
Haiku	405	31.4 percent
BSD	152	11.8 percent
BeOS	83	6.4 percent
Unix (besides BSD)	83	6.4 percent
Other	77	6.0 percent
AmigaOS	37	2.9 percent
ZETA	26	2.0 percent
QNX RTOS	10	0.8 percent
SkyOS	5	0.4 percent

The most used operating systems are Windows, Linux, MacOS, Haiku and BSD. There are almost five times more people that use Haiku than BeOS at least once per week.

Question 6: How many hours have you been using BeOS or Haiku on average per week in the previous 365 days?

If you used both (BeOS and Haiku), then please sum up the times.

Results:

Statistics

BeOSHaikuHoursPerWeekR

N	Valid	1280
	Missing	16
Mean		5.6063
Std. Error of Mean		.38669
Median		1.0000
Mode		.00
Std. Deviation		13.83454

Using BeOS or Haiku (hours per week)

		Frequency	Percent	Valid Percent	Cumulative Percent
Valid	.00	448	34.6	35.0	35.0
	1.00	307	23.7	24.0	59.0
	2.00	128	9.9	10.0	69.0
	3.00	48	3.7	3.8	72.7
	4.00	51	3.9	4.0	76.7
	5.00	45	3.5	3.5	80.2
	6.00	15	1.2	1.2	81.4
	7.00	15	1.2	1.2	82.6
	8.00	15	1.2	1.2	83.8
	9.00	3	.2	.2	84.0
	10.00	56	4.3	4.4	88.4
	13.00	38	2.9	3.0	91.3
	18.00	24	1.9	1.9	93.2
	23.00	16	1.2	1.3	94.5
	28.00	17	1.3	1.3	95.8
	33.00	8	.6	.6	96.4
	38.00	5	.4	.4	96.8
	43.00	3	.2	.2	97.0
	48.00	8	.6	.6	97.7
	53.00	2	.2	.2	97.8
	58.00	3	.2	.2	98.0
	63.00	2	.2	.2	98.2
	68.00	2	.2	.2	98.4
	73.00	1	.1	.1	98.4
	78.00	1	.1	.1	98.5
	88.00	1	.1	.1	98.6
	90.00	18	1.4	1.4	100.0
	Total	1280	98.8	100.0	
Missing	System	16	1.2		
Total		1296	100.0		

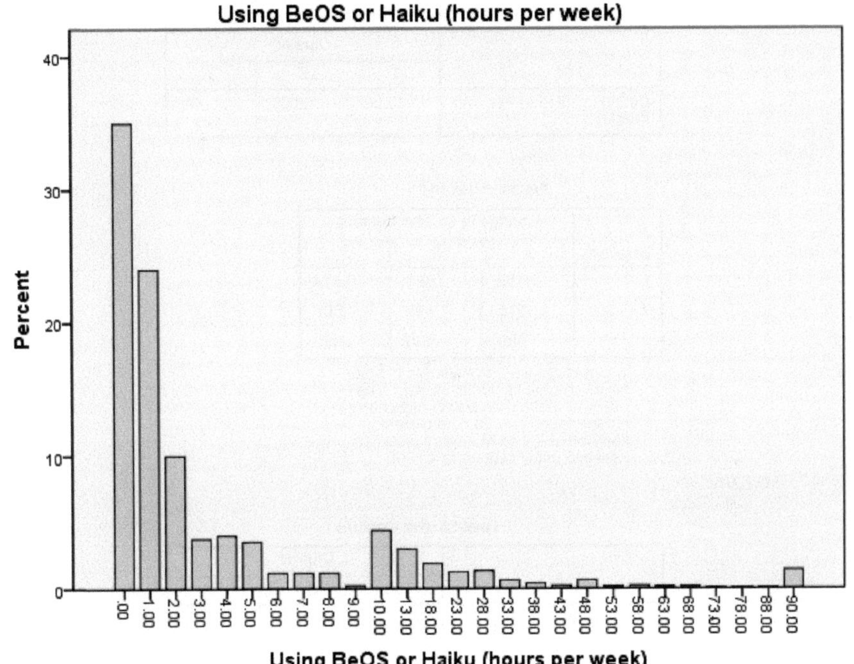

Graphic 20: Survey results regarding the weekly duration of the usage of BeOS or Haiku

The people do not use BeOS respectively Haiku much. The mean duration is equal to 5.6 hours per week. The median is only one hour. The reason for the big difference between the mean and the median is the fact that there are three clusters of people. The biggest cluster (cluster three) consists of persons that do not use Haiku or use it only a little bit (between 0 and 5 hours per week). The next cluster (cluster one) contains people that use it occasionally, the centre of this cluster is at about 34 hours per week. The remaining cluster (cluster two) contains hardcore users. Please note that the value 90 in the chart and the table means "90 or more hours". Therefore the standard deviation is high, equal to about 13.8 hours.

The SPSS 19 syntax used to calculate the clusters:

QUICK CLUSTER BeOSHaikuHoursPerWeekR

 /MISSING=LISTWISE

 /CRITERIA=CLUSTER(3) MXITER(10) CONVERGE(0)

 /METHOD=KMEANS(NOUPDATE)

 /PRINT INITIAL.

Initial Cluster Centers

	Cluster		
	1	2	3
BeOSHaikuHoursPer WeekR	43.00	90.00	.00

Iteration History[a]

	Change in Cluster Centers		
Iteration	1	2	3
1	8.359	3.261	2.484
2	.915	1.899	.000
3	.000	.000	.000

a. Convergence achieved due to no or small change in cluster centers. The maximum absolute coordinate change for any center is .000. The current iteration is 3. The minimum distance between initial centers is 43.000.

Final Cluster Centers

	Cluster		
	1	2	3
BeOSHaikuHoursPer WeekR	33.73	84.84	2.48

Number of Cases in each Cluster

Cluster	1	62.000
	2	25.000
	3	1193.000
Valid		1280.000
Missing		16.000

Graphic 21: Calculated clusters regarding the weekly duration of the usage of BeOS or Haiku

In general, most of the respondents do not use BeOS/Haiku or use it only a little bit, some use it occasionally and a there is a small number of people who belongs to the cluster of hardcore users.

Question 7: If you use Haiku or BeOS, then where do you use it?

Multiple choices are possible.

Results:

Totally, there are 1268 valid results where at least one answer was selected.

At home	984	77.6 percent
At work	87	6.9 percent
At school	45	3.5 percent
Not using	281	22.2 percent

Most people use Haiku respectively BeOS only at home.

Question 8: If you use Haiku, then how do you run it?

Multiple choices are possible.

Results:

Totally, there are 1264 valid results where at least one answer was selected.

Installed on a hard disk partition of a physical computer	554	43.8%
Live CD	140	11.1%
Live USB Stick or other flash memory	169	13.7%
Raw Image used with QEMU	76	6.0%
VM Image run in VMWare or VirtuaBox or an other Virtual Machine	548	43.4%
I do not use Haiku or BeOS	231	18.3%

Popular methods to use Haiku are to install it on a hard disk partition or to use a VM Image.

Question 9: Had you been using BeOS before you became interested in Haiku?

Results:

Totally, there are 1284 valid results where at least one answer was selected.

| Yes. I had used BeOS before I became interested in Haiku. | 889 | 69.2% |
| No. I did not use BeOS before Haiku. I began with Haiku. | 395 | 30.8% |

Most people who are interested in Haiku have experiences with BeOS.

Question 10: When did you begin to use BeOS or Haiku for the first time?

Please note: if you do not know the exact year, please select approximately the year.

Results:

Statistics

SinceWhenBeOSOrHaikuRString

N	Valid	1258
	Missing	38
Mean		2002.7711
Std. Error of Mean		.13570
Median		2003.0000
Mode		1998.00
Std. Deviation		4.81298

Since when using BeOS or Haiku

		Frequency	Percent	Valid Percent	Cumulative Percent
Valid	1993	33	2.5	2.6	2.6
	1998	471	36.3	37.4	40.1
	2003	330	25.5	26.2	66.3
	2006	29	2.2	2.3	68.6
	2007	43	3.3	3.4	72.0
	2008	75	5.8	6.0	78.0
	2009	176	13.6	14.0	92.0
	2010	101	7.8	8.0	100.0
	Total	1258	97.1	100.0	
Missing	System	38	2.9		
Total		1296	100.0		

(Graphic 22: When BeOS respectively Haiku was used for the first time)

The respondents started using BeOS respectively Haiku on average in the year 2003. However, please note that this result is only an estimation because the drop down menu contained classes of years instead of exact years for the period from 1991 to 2005.

<option value="2010">2010</option>   *<option value="2009">2009</option>*

<option value="2008">2008</option>   *<option value="2007">2007</option>*

<option value="2006">2006</option>

<option value="2003">between 2001 and 2005</option>

<option value="1998">between 1996 and 2000</option>

<option value="1993">between 1991 and 1995</option>

Question 11: If you use BeOS or Haiku, then for what purposes?

How often do you use applications in BeOS or Haiku for the following purposes?

Totally 20 purposes were vertically listed and the respondents could give to each of them one of these answers:

never (1), rarely (2), sometimes (3), often (4), very often (5)

Results, ordered by the mean value:

Browsing the web

Mean 3.58   Median 4   Mode 5   Standard deviation 1.35   Valid answers 1086

Internet (general)

Mean 3.45   Median 4   Mode 5   Standard deviation 1.37   Valid answers 1084

Playing music

Mean 3.02   Median 3   Mode 1   Standard deviation 1.48   Valid answers 1064

Playing videos

Mean 2.82   Median 3   Mode 1   Standard deviation 1.46   Valid answers 1049

Writing e-mails

Mean 2.61   Median 2   Mode 1   Standard deviation 1.47   Valid answers 1056

Word processing

Mean 2.09   Median 2   Mode 1   Standard deviation 1.26   Valid answers 1037

Office software

Mean 2.08   Median 2   Mode 1   Standard deviation 1.23   Valid answers 1045

Playing computer games

Mean 1.92   Median 2   Mode 1   Standard deviation 1.11   Valid answers 1025

Other purposes

Mean 1.91   Median 1   Mode 1   Standard deviation 1.33   Valid answers 970

Sound editing

Mean 1.64   Median 1   Mode 1   Standard deviation 1.03   Valid answers 1030

Web design

Mean 1.64   Median 1   Mode 1   Standard deviation 1.07   Valid answers 1026

Web programming

Mean 1.63   Median 1   Mode 1   Standard deviation 1.06   Valid answers 1022

2D design or 2D animation or graphic editing

Mean 1.62   Median 1   Mode 1   Standard deviation 0.99   Valid answers 1036

Music composing or editing

Mean 1.56   Median 1   Mode 1   Standard deviation 0.98   Valid answers 1029

Development or programming of computer games

Mean 1.46   Median 1   Mode 1   Standard deviation 0.95   Valid answers 1021

Web server

Mean 1.46   Median 1   Mode 1   Standard deviation 0.96   Valid answers 1015

Development or programming of HAIKU (kernel, GUI, services, translations, etc.)

Mean 1.45   Median 1   Mode 1   Standard deviation 0.95   Valid answers 1026

Web application server

Mean 1.44   Median 1   Mode 1   Standard deviation 0.92   Valid answers 1022

Development or programming of applications

Mean 1.44   Median 2   Mode 1   Standard deviation 1.42   Valid answers 1022

3D design or 3D animation

Mean 1.26   Median 1   Mode 1   Standard deviation 0.69   Valid answers 1026

If other purposes, please describe them:
MULTILINE TEXTBOX

Among the other purposes often were mentioned these eight ones:

- Testing Haiku in general or features in new nighly builds (95 answers).

- Learning how Haiku or operating systems in general work (32 answers).

- Toying and having fun with Haiku (19 answers).

- Managing files, photographies or videos (11 answers).

- Recording or editing videos (10 answers).

- Communicating by using chats (9 answers).

- Watching TV or listening to radio (8 answers).

- Emulation of other systems (3 answers).

The results show that the people mostly use Haiku respectively BeOS for standard client tasks in the internet, such as browsing the web, writing messages and using chat services, and for playing video or music files. The traditional application areas of the multimedia operating system BeOS, such as editing sounds and videos, composing music or manipulation of 2D and 3D graphics respectively animations, are currently rarely used by the people.

Question 12: How many hours per week do you spend on average for the development (programming, GUI, services, translations, localisations, documentation, community support, etc.) of Haiku?
If you are not developing Haiku, please select 0 hours.
The purpose of this question is to find out how many working hours people contribute in the development of Haiku.

Results:
The valid sample size is 1266 people. Exactly 88 percent of these people do not spend any time for the development of Haiku. Eight percent of the persons spend up to 5 hours per week. The remaining 4 percent of the people spend more than 5 hours per week. About one percent of the respondents spend 20 or even more hours per week (one person spends even 88 hours per week). The mean is equal to about 0.94 hours. The median is 0. The mode is also 0. The standard deviation is equal to about 4.79.

Question 13: Why are you interested in Haiku?

This is a very important question in this survey. Please write a few sentences about your interests and expectations regarding Haiku.

MULTILINE TEXTBOX

Results:

This question was answered by 1147 people. The interpretation of the answers was done manually. Therefore the results are depending on the researcher and can not be exact and sure.

However, such questions where the respondents can freely write what they think are very useful to discover those opinions and arguments that were unknown to the researcher while creating the questions for the survey.

Answer	Number	Percentage
Fan of BeOS or ZETA	360	31.4 percent
Fast booting or very responsive	345	30.1 percent
Simple or easy to use or easy to learn how to use it	263	22.9 percent
Haiku is light	38	12.0 percent
Haiku is free or open source	137	11.9 percent
Interest in desktop operating system	107	9.3 percent
Interest in alternative operating systems in general	100	8.7 percent
Multimedia capabilities	77	6.7 percent
Low hardware requirements	75	6.5 percent
The graphic user interface is nice or clean	70	6.1 percent
Haiku is stable	54	4.7 percent

Other quite often found answers were that Haiku is unified and ready to be used out of the box. There is only one unified distribution and not such a chaos as it exists in Linux.

Some respondents wrote that they like the operating systems AmigaOS or Mac OS and they hope that Haiku will have some features or some of the look and feel of these operating systems.

Question 14: From your point of view, do you agree or disagree regarding these statements?

Totally 13 statements were vertically listed and the respondents could give to each of them one of these answers:

strongly disagree (1), disagree (2), neutral (3), agree (4), strongly agree (5)

Results, ordered by the mean value:

Statement 1: It is important that an operating system supports file sizes of more than 4 GB per file.

Mean 4.22   Median 5   Mode 5   Standard deviation 0.96   Valid answers 1270

Statement 2: One of the most important reasons why I am interested in Haiku is the fast booting of Haiku.

Mean 4.01   Median 4   Mode 4   Standard deviation 0.94   Valid answers 1268

Statement 3: One of the most important reasons why I am interested in Haiku is the user-friendliness (easy to use, user friendly).

Mean 4.00   Median 4   Mode 4   Standard deviation 0.91   Valid answers 1269

Statement 4: One of the most important reasons why I am interested in Haiku is the multimedia performance of Haiku.

Mean 3.95   Median 4   Mode 4   Standard deviation 0.96   Valid answers 1272

Statement 5: One of the most important reasons why I am interested in Haiku are the low hardware requirements.

Mean 3.94   Median 4   Mode 4   Standard deviation 0.97   Valid answers 1262

Statement 6: I am disappointed by Windows because it is too expensive.

Mean 3.89   Median 4   Mode 4   Standard deviation 1.08   Valid answers 1264

Statement 7: I prefer an operating system with a simple graphic user interface (GUI) that supports only essential features, but it is easy to use and very fast.

Mean 3.75   Median 4   Mode 4   Standard deviation 0.98   Valid answers 1264

Statement 8: I dislike Windows because I do not like Microsoft.

Mean 3.19   Median 3   Mode 3   Standard deviation 1.22   Valid answers 1265

Statement 9: I prefer an operating system that is user friendly, even if this means that I can not configure everything in the operating system.

Mean 3.00   Median 3   Mode 4   Standard deviation 1.20   Valid answers 1269

Statement 10: I prefer an operating system that gives me the freedom to configure all possible settings, even if this means that the operating system is not easy to use.

Mean 2.95   Median 3   Mode 3   Standard deviation 1.11   Valid answers 1262

Statement 11: I prefer an operating system with a powerful graphic user interface (GUI) that supports many modern features such as 3D desktop, although this means that the hardware requirements are high.

Mean 2.72   Median 3   Mode 3   Standard deviation 1.08   Valid answers 1266

Statement 12: I am disappointed by Linux because it is too difficult to use.

Mean 2.65   Median 2   Mode 2   Standard deviation 1.27   Valid answers 1265

Statement 13: I am disappointed by Windows because it is too difficult to use.

Mean 2.27   Median 2   Mode 2   Standard deviation 1.10   Valid answers 1264

It is interesting that most people strongly disagree or disagree that Windows is difficult to use (see the statement 13), but many people think that Windows is too expensive (see the statement 6).

The statement 9 is opposite to the statement 10. The mean values of these two statements are not very different (both about 3) and the median values are equal to 3. However, the Pearson correlation coefficient is equal to -0.448 and the correlation is significant at the 0.01 level (the two tailed significance level is 0.000). It seems that there are two clusters of people. Some of them prefer a user friendly operating system with limited opportunities to configure it, others prefer an operating system with much freedom regarding the configuration opportunities, although such an operating system could be difficult to use. However, most of the people choose the answers disagree (2), neutral (3) or agree (4) and not the extreme answers strongly disagree (1) and strongly agree (5).

The statement 7 is opposite to the statement 11. Most of the persons prefer a simple, easy-to-use and fast graphic user interface that supports only essential features. The Pearson correlation coefficient is equal to -0.426 and the correlation is significant at the 0.01 level (the two tailed significance level is 0.000).

In general, many people like Haiku because it is a fast and user-friendly operating system that has low hardware requirements and supports multimedia features, including big files that are often used for video data (see the statements 1 to 5).

Question 15: From your point of view, please prioritise these tasks for the next versions of Haiku. Please note that you can set each level of priority only to one task. The idea is to create a ranking by using each level of priority exactly once.
It is very important that you set a level of priority to every task. Otherwise the ranking will not be complete.

Regarding the analysis of the answers, only those answers, where all tasks got a level of priority, will be taken into account. The resulting sample contains 1009 persons.

Results, first ordered by the median, then ordered by the mean value:

In case of ranks it is normally not allowed to use the mean value because the ranks are based on the ordinal measurement level, but the scale measurement level is required for the usage of the mean. Therefore the median should be used in case of ranks. Sadly, there are two tasks with the median rank 6 respectively two tasks with the median level 4. Therefore the mean value had been also calculated and used as an additional value to determine the ranking, although this is, when being exact, not allowed.

A powerful office software, such as OpenOffice or some other
Mean rank 2.47   Median rank 2   Mode rank 1

A powerful graphic editing software
Mean rank 2.96   Median rank 3   Mode rank 2

A powerful video editing software

Mean rank 3.72   Median rank 4   Mode rank 4

A powerful music composition and sound editing software

Mean rank 3.75   Median rank 4   Mode rank 3

A powerful game development framework for Haiku

Mean rank 4.56   Median rank 5   Mode rank 7

A powerful web application server software

Mean rank 5.21   Median rank 6   Mode rank 6

A powerful web server software

Mean rank 5.32   Median rank 6   Mode rank 7

From the point of view of the people, the most important task is the development or porting of a powerful office software, for example OpenOffice.

A high important task is the development or porting of a powerful software for graphic editing. As already mentioned in previous chapters, there are no professional graphic editing tools, such as latest versions of Adobe Photoshop, for Haiku.

Medium important tasks are the development or porting to powerful video editing software respectively music composition and sound editing software.

As already mentioned in previous chapters, Haiku is a desktop operating system. Therefore it is no wonder, that web application server software respectively web server software are not important from the point of view of many people.

Question 16: How old are you? (years)

Statistics

AgeR

N	Valid	1280
	Missing	16
Mean		30.9898
Std. Error of Mean		.25875
Median		30.0000
Mode		30.00
Std. Deviation		9.25737

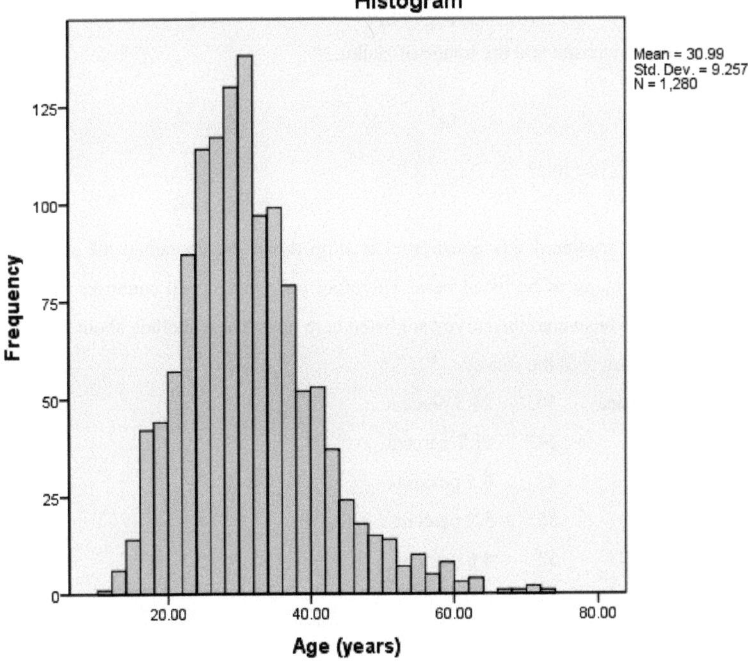

Graphic 23: Age in years

Totally 1280 persons answered this question. On average the respondents are 31 (mean) respectively 30 (median) years old. The standard deviation is equal to about 9.26 years. Most of the respondents (about 78 percent) are between 20 and 40 years old.

Question 17: What is your gender?

O Female   O Male

Results:

Totally 1274 persons answered this question. Only 11 (0.9 percent) of the respondents are female. There are about 115 times more males then females. Haiku is still an exotic operating system that is mostly interesting for people who are fascinated by technology and computer sciences. In such fields females are rare in general.

However, such a huge lack of females in this survey is very surprising. One reason may be that many fans of Haiku were fans of BeOS in past. In the previous century there was only a very small percentage of females among computer users. Nevertheless, even this can not totally explain this huge lack of female respondents in this survey.

Perhaps the Haiku community should try to become more fascinating for females by doing some changes regarding the website and the image of Haiku.

Question 18: Where do you live?

Results:

Totally 1256 persons answered this question. The drop down list contained all countries of the world. There are too many to be listed here. Therefore only the top 10 countries ordered by the number of people who answered the survey are listed here now. These include about 67.9 percent of all the persons who answered the survey.

United States of America	305	24.3 percent
Germany	147	11.7 percent
United Kingdom	82	6.5 percent
France	65	5.2 percent
Canada	58	4.6 percent
Sweden	44	3.5 percent
Netherlands	41	3.3 percent
Australia	39	3.1 percent
Italy	39	3.1 percent
Poland	33	2.6 percent

Question 19: What is your current occupation?

Results:

Occupation

		Frequency	Percent	Valid Percent	Cumulative Percent
Valid	No answer	40	3.1	3.1	3.1
	Artist	16	1.2	1.2	4.3
	Employee	519	40.0	40.0	44.4
	Entrepreneur	65	5.0	5.0	49.4
	Freelancer	118	9.1	9.1	58.5
	Homemaker	3	.2	.2	58.7
	Military	5	.4	.4	59.1
	Musician	6	.5	.5	59.6
	Other	111	8.6	8.6	68.1
	Public	22	1.7	1.7	69.8
	Scientist	53	4.1	4.1	73.9
	Student (college)	34	2.6	2.6	76.5
	Student (high school)	57	4.4	4.4	80.9
	Student (university)	190	14.7	14.7	95.6
	Unemployed	57	4.4	4.4	100.0
	Total	1296	100.0	100.0	

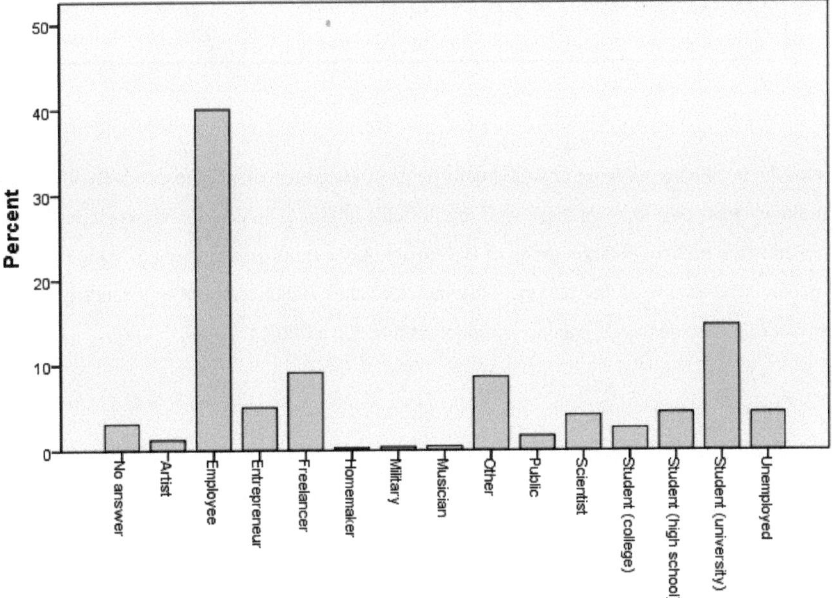

Graphic 24: Occupation

Question 20: What is your current field of work or study?

If you have more than one field, then please choose the field that is most important for you.

Results:

Field of work

		Frequency	Percent	Valid Percent	Cumulative Percent
Valid	Agriculture	9	.7	.7	.7
	Arts, graphics, multimedia	57	4.4	4.4	5.1
	Business or economics	49	3.8	3.8	8.9
	Computer sciences or IT	791	61.0	61.0	69.9
	Construction, architecture	26	2.0	2.0	71.9
	Handcraft	6	.5	.5	72.4
	Human sciences	34	2.6	2.6	75.0
	Life sciences	22	1.7	1.7	76.7
	Literature, languages, writing, translations etc.	19	1.5	1.5	78.2
	Machinery engineering	39	3.0	3.0	81.2
	Music or sound	17	1.3	1.3	82.5
	Natural sciences	53	4.1	4.1	86.6
	No answer	47	3.6	3.6	90.2
	Other	123	9.5	9.5	99.7
	Sports	4	.3	.3	100.0
	Total	1296	100.0	100.0	

Graphic 25: Field of work

Most of the people are working or studying in fields of computer sciences respectively information technology. Other people, even those working in fields of arts, graphics, sound, music respectively multimedia (the traditional target group of BeOS) are only a small group (about 5.7 percent) among the people who answered the survey. This indicates that Haiku and BeOS are not playing an important role in professional graphic, sound or multimedia editing.

Question 21: What is your highest degree (education)?

If your degree is missing in the list, then please choose a degree that is similar to yours degree.

Results:

Education

		Frequency	Percent	Valid Percent	Cumulative Percent
Valid	No answer	35	2.7	2.7	2.7
	Associate degree	40	3.1	3.1	5.8
	Bachelor	323	24.9	24.9	30.7
	Certificate of Higher Education	54	4.2	4.2	34.9
	German Diplom (FH)	20	1.5	1.5	36.4
	German Diplom (Uni)	31	2.4	2.4	38.8
	Doctorate	38	2.9	2.9	41.7
	High school	232	17.9	17.9	59.6
	Magister	5	.4	.4	60.0
	Master	192	14.8	14.8	74.8
	Middle school	55	4.2	4.2	79.1
	Other	82	6.3	6.3	85.4
	Post doctorate	6	.5	.5	85.9
	Some other four years college or university degree	57	4.4	4.4	90.3
	Some other three years college or university degree	50	3.9	3.9	94.1
	Some other two years college or university degree	54	4.2	4.2	98.3
	Undergraduate degree	22	1.7	1.7	100.0
	Total	1296	100.0	100.0	

Graphic 26: Education

When looking at the above listed education levels of the people, then it is not easy to determine the average level of education because there are many very different degrees, depending on the type of school and the differences between the education systems in various countries.

However, these education levels can be ordered within a ranking list. Of course, I am aware of the problems which appear when trying to create a ranking by comparing different degrees and school system from different countries. Often it is not easy to make a decision and some of the decisions may be not correct from some points of view. For example, I did not make differences between a Bachelor degree and a Bachelor degree honours, although there is a difference between these two degrees in the United Kingdom. Therefore this SPSS RECODE statement is just a approximation that does not create a perfect ranking, but the created ranking is sufficient for the purpose of estimating an average level of education of the people who answered this survey.

RECODE Education (MISSING=SYSMIS) ('?'=SYSMIS) ('Middle school'=1) ('High school'=2) ('CHE'=3) ('ASH'=4) ('SomeOtherTwoYears'=4) ('UGD'=4) ('Bachelor'=5) ('SomeOtherThreeYears'=5) ('DiplomFH'=5) ('SomeOtherFourYears'=5) ('Magister'=6) ('Master'=6) ('DiplomUni'=6) ('Doctorate'=7) ('Post doctorate'=8) ('Other'=SYSMIS) INTO EducationR. EXECUTE.

Both, the median value and the mode value are equal to 5 which means that on average the people who answered the survey have a Bachelor degree or some other more or less similar degree that required between three and four years of studying at a university or college.

Question 22: What is your marital status?

Results:

This question was answered by 1236 people. About 27.8 percent are married. Additionally, about 26.9 percent are not married, but they have a romantic relationship or are engaged. About 0.3 percent are widows. The most frequently chosen option, to be exact 45.0 percent, was the marital status Single. An interesting question is how many people are in any kind of romantic relation and how many are without a partner. This was done by using this SPSS syntax:

RECODE MartialStatus (MISSING=SYSMIS) ('?'=SYSMIS) ('Single'=0) ('Widowed'=0) ('UnmarriedButWithPartner'=1) ('Married'=1) INTO MartialStatusR.
EXECUTE.

Totally only 54.7 percent have a partner. This is less than the average in most western countries. In general, many of the people who answered the survey are single.

Question 23: How many children do you have?

Results:

This question was answered by 1244 people. Both, the mode and median values are equal to zero. The mean is about 0.44 and the standard deviation is equal to about 0.90. About 76 percent of the persons have no children. About 10 percent have one child and another 10 percent have two children. About 4 percent have three or more children.

Question 24: If you like, you can enter your e-mail address in the free text field. This is only OPTIONAL and by doing this, you accept possible further questions about your opinion regarding Haiku or BeOS via e-mail.

If you do not like any further questions, please leave this text field blank.

E-mail address (optional): ONELINE TEXTFIELD

Results:

Totally there are 496 persons that entered an e-mail address. Within the first few weeks of the survey some of them (less than 50) were contacted regarding additional information for the questions 3 and 4 of the survey because many had chosen the answer "other" operating system. Their answers were used to manually update the data sets in the survey and add additional entries (operating systems) in the drop down list of the survey.

6.2.2. Correlations

First of all, it is wise to check whether the survey data is valid and useful for the calculation and interpretation of correlations. An easy way to do this is to take a look at the socio-demographic data. In general, a positive correlation between age and number of children can be expected. Furthermore, people who are married or in a long term relationship have on average more children than people who are single.

These two general expectations can be verified with the correlation coefficients that were calculated by using the survey data:

The Pearson correlation coefficient between age and number of children is equal to 0.461 and the level of significance is equal to 0.000 (N=1239). The Pearson correlation coefficient between the recoded MartialStatusR (see the question 22 in the chapter 6.2.1) and the age is equal to 0.397 and the level of significance is equal to 0.000 (N=1225).

These results show that the data seems to be valid and useful for the calculation and analyses of correlations.

Result: Old people prefer user-friendly operating systems

There is a weak, but highly significant, correlation between the number of children and the importance of user-friendliness regarding operating systems (see statement 9 regarding the question 14 in the chapter 6.2.1).

The Pearson correlation coefficient between age and number of children is equal to 0.110 and the level of significance is equal to 0.000 (N=1223). At first sight the reason for this may be that many people who have children want to spend a part of their free time with them and therefore they neither have the time nor the motivation to spend dozens of hours to learn how to use a complicated operating system. However, this is only a an illusion because there is a strong correlation between the age and the number of children (the Pearson correlation coefficient is equal to 0.461 and the significance level is equal to 0.000). In fact, the age of the people is the relevant variable regarding the importance of user-friendliness of operating systems. In order to eliminate the influence of the age regarding the correlation between the number of children and the importance of user-friendliness of operating systems, the age was used as the control variable in a partial correlation calculation. In this case the correlation between the number of children and the importance of user-friendliness regarding operating systems is only 0.044 and the correlation is not significant (significance level is equal to 0.124). However, when using the number of children as the control variable, we see a significant correlation between the age and the the importance of user-friendliness regarding operating systems (variable *OSShallBeUFR*). Furthermore, there are significant correlations between the age and the variables *Linux is difficult* (see the statement 12 regarding the question 14 in the chapter 6.2.1) respectively *importance of supporting big files* (see the statement 1 regarding the question 14 in the chapter 6.2.1).

In general, it seems to be that the older the people are, the more they think that Linux is difficult and an operating system shall be user friendly. However, the correlation coefficients are quite small.

Correlations

Control Variables			AgeR	OSShall BeUFR	Linux DifficultR	Big FilesR
ChildrenR	AgeR	Correlation	1.000	.123	.127	-.173
		Significance (2-tailed)	.	.000	.000	.000
		df	0	1209	1209	1209
	OSShallBeUFR	Correlation	.123	1.000	.379	-.026
		Significance (2-tailed)	.000	.	.000	.374
		df	1209	0	1209	1209
	LinuxDifficultR	Correlation	.127	.379	1.000	.003
		Significance (2-tailed)	.000	.000	.	.923
		df	1209	1209	0	1209
	BigFilesR	Correlation	-.173	-.026	.003	1.000
		Significance (2-tailed)	.000	.374	.923	.
		df	1209	1209	1209	0

Graphic 27: Correlations regarding age

Result: Fans of BeOS and Haiku do not hate Microsoft and Windows

There is no significant respectively no worthy of mention correlation between the level of interest in BeOS respectively Haiku and the variables WindowsExpensiveR, DislikeMicrosoftR, WindowsDifficultR and (see the statement 6, 8 and 13 regarding the question 14 in the chapter 6.2.1). The levels of significance are worse than 0.05 or the Pearson correlation coefficient is between -0.10 and +0.10. But there is a weak correlation between the variable LinuxDifficult and the level of interest in BeOS. The Pearson correlation is equal to 0.151 and the level of significance is equal to 0.000 (N=1259). However, this is only a weak correlation.

In general, there seems to be no correlation between the level of interest in BeOS respectively Haiku and the sympathy for other operating systems. A hostility, such as between many Linux fans and Microsoft Windows, seems not to exists in the Haiku community.

Result: Fans of BeOS and Haiku like the simplicity, speed, multimedia features and low hardware requirements of these operating systems

There are highly significant, to be precious all the significance levels are equal to 0.000, correlations (Pearson correlation coefficients between 0.212 and 0.293) between the level of interest in Haiku (InterestedInHaikuR) respectively BeOS (InterestedInBeOSR) and the reason why the people are interested in Haiku (see the corresponding statements regarding the question 14 in the chapter 6.2.1): ReasonHaikuSimpleR (statement 3), ReasonHaikuFastR (statement 2), ReasonHaikuMultimediaR (statement 4), ReasonHaikuLowHardwareReqR (statement 5).

Pearson Correlation Coefficient	InterestedInHaikuR	InterestedInBeOSR
InterestedInHaikuR	1.000 (N=1291)	0.531 (N=1285)
ReasonHaikuSimpleR	0.293 (N=1261)	0.279 (N=1263)
ReasonHaikuFastR	0.216 (N=1266)	0.216 (N=1263)
ReasonHaikuMultimediaR	0.266 (N=1270)	0.292 (N=1266)
ReasonHaikuLowHardwareReqR	0.212 (N=1260)	0.214 (N=1256)

These four reasons were also often given answers regarding the question 13 where the people could freely write in a multi-line text box. Therefore a conclusion is that these four characteristics of Haiku are key features from the point of view of many fans and users of Haiku respectively BeOS.

Result: The marital status and level of education of the members of the Haiku community play no worth of mention role regarding the interest for Haiku and the reasons why they are fascinated by Haiku.

There are no mentionable correlations between the socio-demographic variables marital status and the level of education on the one hand and the variables InterestedInHaikuR and all the reasons why the people are interested in Haiku on the other hand. Whether there are some correlations between these variables and the gender can not be said because only 11 of 1274 people are female in the survey.

6.3. Summary

Although the respondents answered that their favourit operating system is Haiku respectively BeOS, the most often used operating system family is Microsoft Windows (see the results corresponding to the questions 1 to 5 in the chapter 6.2.1).

On average the people use Haiku less than 6 hours per week. When calculating the median instead of the mean, then it is even only one hour per week (see the results corresponding to the question 6 in the chapter 6.2.1).

In general, the respondents use Haiku respectively BeOS at home and very rarely at school or at work (see the results corresponding to the question 7 in the chapter 6.2.1).

When they use Haiku, then it is mostly installed on a hard disk partition of a physical computer or it is used as a VM image run in a virtual machine (see the results corresponding to the question 8 in the chapter 6.2.1).

More than two-thirds of all people answered that they had used BeOS before they became interested in Haiku (see the results corresponding to the question 9 in the chapter 6.2.1). This means that Haiku did not gain many new users and fans. It could be necessary to improve the marketing activities.

When using Haiku or BeOS, most people use applications that are typical for desktop computing, such as browsing the web, playing music, playing videos and internet in general (see the results corresponding to the question 11 in the chapter 6.2.1).

Many people are interested in Haiku because they are fans of BeOS or ZETA. Other often given reasons are the booting speed, the responsiveness, the ease of use and the facts that Haiku is light and free (see the results corresponding to the questions 13 and 14 in the chapter 6.2.1).

The respondents think that the most important tasks for the next version of Haiku shall be the development or porting of a powerful office software and a powerful graphic editing software (see the results corresponding to the question 15 in the chapter 6.2.1). These results are no wonder because there exists no worthy of mention office software for Haiku. The old office software products available for BeOS are not compatible with Haiku. The most powerful available graphic editing tool is WonderBrush. Although this graphic editing software is useful for small private projects and supports layers, it is not powerful enough to be used for professional graphic editing and can not enter the competition with GIMP or Adobe Photoshop.

Almost all Haiku users are male. Less than one percent of the people, that answered the survey, are female. Most of the people are about 30 years old, have a high level of education and work in fields of computer sciences or information technology. Quite many are singles and about three-fourths have no children (see the results corresponding to the questions 16 to 23 in the chapter 6.2.1).

The older the people are, the more they appreciate user friendly operating systems and the more they think, that Linux is difficult to use.
Most fans of BeOS respectively Haiku do not hate Microsoft. There seems to be no hostility regarding Microsoft or Windows, in opposite to the situation in the Linux community where such a hostility exists.
In general, the fans of Haiku respectively BeOS appreciate the speed, simplicity, low hardware requirements and multimedia features of these two operating systems (see the bivariate correlations and partial correlations in the chapter 6.2.2).

C. Conclusion and further thoughts

At the moment it is difficult to say whether Haiku will be successful or not. The latest version is still an Alpha release and therefore it does not contain all the features that are planned for the final release. However, even the current Alpha release has some characteristics that are very appreciated by the Haiku community. The most important of these characteristics are the speed, responsiveness, ease of use and lightness of Haiku. These characteristics are important for desktop operating systems and the results of the survey show that the Haiku community is appreciating exactly these features of Haiku. Even the Alpha releases of Haiku are much faster regarding booting times and responsiveness than most modern operating systems. From the point of view of ease of use, Haiku is exemplary and largely fulfils the ISO 9241-11 ergonomic requirements.

The most serious problem of Haiku is the lack of available applications. Currently there does not exist even one worth of mention office software for Haiku. But a powerful office software is one of the most important applications for any desktop operating system. Similar problems occur regarding other types of software, such as graphic editing tools and modern video editing tools.

An other serious problem is the lack of drivers for modern hardware, especially for graphic cards. Currently Haiku supports only some old NVidia and ATI graphic cards by using native drivers. In all other cases only VESA drivers are available. This is a situation that has to be changed as soon as possible, especially when considering that BeOS was called the Multimedia Operating System and Haiku tries to be a successful successor of it.

It is not easy to say whether Haiku will be widely used or remain only an operating system used by a small number of very loyal and enthusiastic BeOS fans.

From my point of view, Haiku could have the best chances to become successful in the netbook market. Haiku is fast, simple, light and very user friendly. Furthermore, Haiku has low hardware requirements and this is an important feature for all operating systems meant to be used for netbooks. Currently there is a project for porting Haiku to the ARM platform. Some analysts believe that ARM processors could become an interesting alternative to x86 compatible processors in the netbook market because of the low costs and high energy efficiency of ARM based platforms. Here Haiku could become an interesting operating system because it is fast, free and has low hardware requirements.

Furthermore, there are not many competitors regarding operating systems for ARM based platforms. Until now there is only a small number of netbooks based on ARM architecture, for example the Toshiba AC100, and these mostly use the operating system Google Android which is optimized for smartphones with touch screens, but not for netbooks. Here Haiku could become a strong player in the market.

Haiku requires only a Pentium or better CPU, at least 128 MB RAM and 600 MB of storage space on the hard disk. If there were an ARM port of Haiku, it could perform excellently on ARM based netbooks, such as one with a 1 GHz ARM CPU, for example the ARM Coretex-A9 MPCore, 512 MB RAM, a small Solid State Disc and corresponding multimedia devices (integrated graphic and sound processing).

Such a netbook could cost less than 200 Euro, yet have the capabilities to play high quality audio and video records and let the user do most of the daily tasks that are important for netbooks, for example using the internet, editing some photos for personal profiles in social networks and creating some amateur graphics that do not require professional software such as Adobe Photoshop. Haiku could become a very responsive, fast booting and user friendly operating system that has a focus on the purpose of netbooks: personal computing.

Bibliography and other sources

When internet sources are listed, then the at the end of the line written date is the date of the access to the website. The date of the creation or editing of the information is often unknown. If it is known, then it is additionally mentioned in the source.

ACCESS Co., Ltd., Be Inc.: The Be Book, in the internet:
http://www.haiku-os.org/legacy-docs/bebook, Date: 10th August 2010

Berka, Stefan (2004 to 2010): Operating System Reviews (History, Facts, Versions and Screenshots),
in the internet: www.operating-system.org, Date: 14th November 2010

BlueEyedOS (2001 to 2003): BlueEyedOS,
in the internet: http://www.blueeyedos.com, Date: 14th November 2010

Böhle, Fritz: Softwareentwicklung als Arbeits- und Organisationsgestaltung – Softwareergonomie, Extraordinat für Sozioökonomie der Arbeits- und Berufswelt, WiSo Fakultät, Universität Augsburg, chapter I.1, the publication year is unknown, perhaps about 2000. (GERMAN)

Bühl Achim (2010): SPSS 18 – Einführung in die moderne Datenanalyse, 12th revised edition, Pearson Studium, Munich, Germany (GERMAN)

Card K, Stuart / Mackinlay D., Jock , Shneiderman, Ben (1999): Readings in Information Visualization: Using Vision to Think, Academic Press, San Diego, California, United States of America

Drinkwater, John (2006): Haiku kernel diagram,
in the internet: http://ezri.nextraweb.com, Date: 11th August 2010

Yoder, Jon (2010): Learning to Program with Haiku, Lulu.com, Raleigh, California, United States of America

Giampaolo, Dominic (1999): Practical File System Design with the Be File System, Morgan Kaufmann Publishers, INC., San Francisco, California, United States of America

Golftheman: Monolith-, Micro- and a "hybrid" kernel, a draft of new version, a diagram from the Wikimedia Commons, created or last update: 17th July 2008.
In the internet: http://en.wikipedia.org/wiki/File:OS-structure2.svg

Haikuware: Website bebits.com, in the internet: http://wiki.bebits.com/page/BeOsReleases,
          Date: 23rd July 2010

Sydow, Dan Parks: Programming the Be Operating System, O'Reilly & Associate, Sebastopol, California, United States of America

Rey, Günter Daniel: E-Learning, Cognitive Load Theory, in the internet:
http://www.elearning-psychologie.de/clt.html, Date: 26th June 2010 (GERMAN)

Hacker, Scot / Bortman, Henry / Herborth, Chris (1999): The BeOS Bible, Peachpit Press, Berkeley, California, United States of America

Haiku, Inc. (2001 to 2010): The official website about the Haiku Project,
in the internet: http://www.haiku-os.org

Haikuware (1999 to 2010): Website bebits.com, in the internet: http://wiki.bebits.com

Haikuware (2007 to 2010): Software for Haiku, in the internet: http://haikuware.com

Leavengood (2008-07-14): Laying It All Out, Part 1,
article in the internet: http://www.haiku-os.org/documents/dev/laying_it_all_out_part_1,
Date: 14th November 2010

magnussoft Deutschland (R) GmbH (2006 to 2007): ZETA-OS,
in the internet: http://www.zeta-os.com, Date: 14th November 2010

Stippi: Why Haiku Vector Icons are So Small, article in:
http://www.haiku-os.org/articles/2009-09-14_why_haiku_vector_icons_are_so_small,
Date: 24th July 2010

The Be Development Team (1998): Advanced Topics, O'Reilly & Associates, Sebastopol,
California, United States of America

The Be Development Team (1997): Be Developer's Guide, O'Reilly & Associates, Sebastopol,
California, United States of America

Toyomasu, Kei Grieg: HAIKU for PEOPLE, in the internet: http://www.toyomasu.com/haiku,
last updated: 10th January 2001, Date: 14th August 2010

Tücke, Manfred (2003): Grundlagen der Psychologie für (zukünftige) Lehrer, pages 160 to 179, LIT
Verlag Münster (GERMAN)

Yoder, Jon (2010): Learning to program with Haiku, Lulu Enterprises, Inc., Raleigh, North
California, United States of America

Wikipedia: http://en.wikipedia.org/wiki/Hybrid_kernel, Date: 25th July 2010

Wikipedia: http://en.wikipedia.org/wiki/Microkernel, Date: 25th July 2010

Wikipedia: http://en.wikipedia.org/wiki/Monolithic_kernel, Date: 24th July 2010

Disclaimer of warranty

The author and the publisher of this book have made their best efforts to provide a high quality and fascinating book. However, it is possible that there are mistakes, not complete or not up-to-date information in this book. Please note that Haiku is still under development and the features of the operating systems may change every day. No guarantee, comment or warranties of any kind are made with regard to the accuracy, actuality, applicability, correctness, fitness or completeness of the contents of this book.

The author and the publisher disclaim any warranties of any kind for any purpose.

Neither the author nor the publisher accept any liability of any kind for any damages or losses that are caused or supposed to be caused (directly or indirectly) from using any information, opinion or comment that is available in this book.